"Nader Elguindi is no victim[...] he's chosen to overcome. And his s[...] pull tears from your eyes. Nader chose to live. And those of us lucky enough to know him and know his story are all better for it."

Cam Marston, President, Marston Communications, Charlotte, N.C.

"In My Decision to Live, Nader records for us his difficult moments, fears and, most importantly, his belief in himself to pull through and create a great life - one well worth living fully. A must read for anyone who's acquired a disability along life's path."

John D. Kemp, Esq., Author & Professional Speaker, Washington, D.C.

"Nader has the unique ability to draw us into his amazing story, where we find ourselves and our own story in the context of his triumph."

Lou Solomon, Owner, Interact Skills LLC, Charlotte, N.C.

"Most of us are given the gift of life only once. Nader Elguindi received the gift of life a second time and embraced it with vigor. His memoir recounts turning a would-be tragedy into a triumph, by choosing life and living it to its fullest."

Barbara Laughlin, Retired, CIO First Union National Bank

"Each of us faces difficult struggles in our lives...if we are lucky they will pale in comparison to Nader's story. I think we all can learn, find encouragement and re-dedicate ourselves from the true story within these pages."

Todd A. Weiler, Former Principal Deputy Assistant Secretary of the Army

"Nader Elguindi is an American hero. His grit and determination will inspire you just as it inspired the crew of the nuclear submarine we served on together. After being told his severe injuries would prevent him from continued Naval service, Lieutenant Elguindi went on to earn the coveted gold dolphins for qualifying in submarines. His story is an inspiration and testament to his faith for anyone facing challenges."

Rear Admiral Mark Kenny, Commander, Center for Submarine Counter-terrorism Operations and Former USS *Birmingham* Commanding Officer.

My Decision to Live

Story of the first U.S. Naval Officer to earn his
submarine qualifications with a prosthetic leg

Nader Elguindi

Rick,

Thanks for supporting
our troops! It was
an honor to work with
G Attn.

Best,
Nad

Elguindi, Nader
My Decision to Live / Nader Elguindi
p.cm.
ISBN -10: 1-58776-857-7
ISBN -13: 978-1-58776-857-6

Library of Congress Control Number: 2006939957

Printed on acid-free paper
Manufactured in the United States of America
10 9 8 7 6 5 4 3 2

Books are available in quantity for promotional or premise use. To order additional copies please contact us:
Cydecor, Inc.
300 North Lee Street, Suite 302
Alexandria, VA 22209
orders@cydecor.com

**HUDSON
HOUSE**

675 Dutchess Turnpike, Poughkeepsie, NY 12603
www.hudsonhousepub.com (800) 724-1100

DEDICATION

This book is dedicated to all the troops at Walter Reed Army Medical Center as well as the many other military medical centers that serve our country. These men and women have suffered incredible injuries and often loss of limbs in support of our freedom. Their bravery, unselfishness and most of all, incredible willpower, inspire me more than words can express.

All of the proceeds from this book go toward the non-profits that support our Wounded Warriors at Walter Reed.

ACKNOWLEDGEMENTS

First and foremost, I want to thank my coach, Lou Solomon. Lou is a special person in my life and my professional speaking coach. With her encouragement, I developed the framework of this book. Without her, this book would never have been finished. Lou, thank you very much.

I want to thank my sister, Nellie. Without her support and encouragement I would not have been able to recover as quickly, gain the necessary confidence to go back, or start my successful business. Although she and I are not always on the same page, I will forever believe that we are twins split from the same genes.

To my mom and dad, I owe a debt of gratitude for bringing me into this world. From my dad, I learned the meaning of passion and the relentless strive for perfection. From my mom, compassion despite adversity. Both have formed who I am today.

My ultimate indebtedness is to the doctors, nurses and supporting staff of Tripler Army Medical Center in Hawaii who resurrected my body and life and helped put humpty dumpty back together again. Special thanks to Dr. Craig Ono for putting my legs back together so I could have a chance to walk again.

Rear Admiral Mark W. Kenny, my mentor, true life role model, and always my Captain. In addition to Mark there are the many shipmates and entire crew of the USS *Birmingham* (SSN-695). Certainly a special tribute to Ed Meintzer, whose bravery and unselfish support was a guide for me on that fateful night and who is a friend for life.

Rear Admiral Engelhardt and the staff of Submarine Squadron Seven, who all made it possible for me to pave new roads and remain on active duty as long as I did.

Pastor Ray Villiamu and everyone at Makakilo Baptist Church in Makakilo, Hawaii - a place I still consider home to this day.

Of course, thank you to the many, many dear friends who helped me along the way: Cam Martson, Andy Dinkin, Kal Kardous, Matthew Belk, Tom Bojarski, Chris Long, and so many more that they wouldn't fit on this page.

To my best friend, Anne, to whom I cannot measure my gratitude.

To God, for giving me the chance to succeed and a second chance at life.

INTRODUCTION

This book is meant to be inspirational and I hope you will feel stronger and more excited about life having read it. I have been very fortunate in my life and personally embrace a quote by Booker T. Washington that says, "Success is to be measured not so much by the position that one has reached in life as by the obstacles which he has overcome." My adversities have formed who I am today, and I am publicizing my story because I believe the need to overcome challenges and make good choices faces all of us. I believe we all have one gift we are given as men and women: choice. Choice forms our attitude and our attitude forms the path to our future. Think positively and positive outcomes will come, eventually. Life is about persistence and patience, and everything has a way of working out in the end.

TABLE OF CONTENTS

STAGE ONE:
REALITY HITS

CHAPTER I
- THE ACCIDENT -

Most of our lives are spent in habitual activities. We remember general patterns - such as how we go to work or what we usually eat for lunch - but the particulars of individual days tend to blur into each other. Some days, however, are frozen in time. Crystallized. The sights, sounds, smells, and gut sensation of those moments are tangible realities, even years afterward. One of those moments for me was when I woke up on November 22, 1994. When I came back to consciousness, lying in a hospital bed, my life changed entirely.

The lights were low, and I felt as if I were looking through a light fog, my eyes bleary from having been closed for so long. I could hear a steady, mechanical beeping in the room. It gradually synchronized with the clock's ticking, then eased back out, like a movement of waves. I wasn't sure if I was alive or dead. I blinked a few times to clear my vision and surveyed my surroundings. There were monitors all around me, and tubes were going in and out of my mouth and chest. I felt like I was on a movie set and was waiting for someone to explain my role.

My gaze drifted to the foot of my bed, and I suddenly realized that my parents were standing there together. It was then that I knew something terrible must have happened. Not only had I not seen my mom since college graduation two years ago, or my dad in more than five years, but this was the first time in eighteen years I'd seen them together. They had divorced when I was young, and over the years my relationship with both of them had become strained.

While I was still digesting the view of my parents together and feeling frustrated that I couldn't gather the energy or focus to say anything to them, I heard footsteps, and a tall man in a white lab coat appeared at the side of my hospital bed. He put his hand on my shoulder and, with effort, I rolled my eyes to look into his. "Son, you've been in a terrible accident and you're lucky to be alive." *Lucky.* It rang in my head like an echo in a long, dark tunnel. How in the world was this luck? Was he out of his mind? I felt a brief, electric wave of panic run through my body.

But this quickening of reality soon faded, along with my sense of alarm, to a more general state of hazy confusion. I had been given heavy doses of morphine, and my attention drifted easily, from a vague worry about what might have happened, to processing my world, now a hospital room. Passing through time felt like drifting through a dark ocean. My parents left the room, then came back. Nurses and doctors went in and out. I couldn't comprehend what might have been so terrible that it brought my mom and dad together here with me, and eventually I just lay there wondering when I could leave and go back home, wherever that might be. It was only later that I heard what had happened to me and understood how right the doctor was. I was lucky.

***

At 5 a.m. on Sunday, November 20, 1994, a couple driving down H-1 Freeway on the Hawaiian island of Oahu saw a motorcycle lying on its side in the right-hand shoulder of the freeway. The headlamp was lit and facing oncoming traffic. Puzzled, the couple stopped their car on the side of the road and got out. Seeing no one around, they climbed a mound and discovered me lying on the ground, barely conscious but alive. Both my legs were severed below the knee and there was blood everywhere. My motorcycle had collided violently with an exit sign at freeway speed, crushing my lower body and tossing me over the hill.

They dialed 911 on their mobile phone. There was a small hospital just two miles away, but when the ambulance arrived my situation was too dire to make the twenty-minute haul to the nearest trauma center. The call went out for an emergency helicopter. Arriving at Tripler Army Medical Center, I underwent more than eighteen hours of emergency surgery, during which both legs were reattached. Only my head - I had a helmet on - and right arm had been spared from injury. I endured two legs reattached below the knees, one broken femur, severed nerves in my left arm, and internal injuries that required the removal of my appendix. Fortunately, the drugs and shock erased my memory of those hours.

I often think about that night and all that had to happen for me to be alive today. The couple could have easily driven on without stopping - it was a remote part of the island where cars were few and far between at that hour, they had had a few drinks that night, and it was late and dark outside. They could have wondered briefly what the motorcycle was doing there, then gone home. The odds of them having a mobile phone were also not high. Although you can hardly find a person nowadays who doesn't have a mobile phone, back in 1994 they were a rarity. And the medical response and availability of resources were fast and excellent - my life hinged on a fine point, and the medical teams who helped me that night tipped the scale back in my favor. Unfortunately, the police report held no record of the couple's names, so I wondered if I would ever get to thank the people who had helped save my life. Even a call and a visit to the police officer who had written the report provided only sketchy details about the couple and no identifying information.

Chapter 2
- Waking Up -

When I first woke up, I couldn't feel a thing - my entire body was numb. But as the medication began to wear off, a dull pain started to creep through my body. My legs ached. I couldn't get my left arm to do even simple movements. Everything started to hurt and I felt like I had been hurled down an abandoned well.

Two days earlier, I had been an up-and-coming lieutenant on the USS *Birmingham*, a U.S. Navy submarine stationed in Pearl Harbor. I remember lying in my hospital bed, trying with what energy I could muster to focus on what had happened before the accident. I could recall revving up my motorcycle after the night shift aboard the submarine in Pearl Harbor, Hawaii, where we had just completed a major nuclear maintenance procedure. A cool breeze swept across my face as I cruised along the familiar freeway heading home. But that was all - everything from that up to the moment when I woke up in Tripler hospital was gone from my memory.

Eventually, the gravity of my situation began to seep in. The reality registered little by little. I reached out to God for strength. I had done this for several years, but this time it was different: I could have died that day, but I didn't. I was spared for a reason; one that would fuel my will to continue and to live, even today.

For the next few days, doctors and nurses monitored my status hourly. My right leg was in terrible condition. In fact, it was hardly a leg anymore - only a rough, thin bone ran the full length of my calf, the flesh bunched around it in raw knots. At the ankle, there were splinters of bone jutting out, and only a thin strip of skin continued from the calf to the foot, carrying with it one precious blood vessel that continued to bring blood to my foot, which was a deep purple color. The left leg was crushed at the ankle but at least the skin and muscle were still there. The impact of the accident had jettisoned my left talus, the small ball-shaped bone that sits between the leg and ankle parts of the foot. Both legs were being held together by metal pins, and neither was in good enough condition for a cast. All they could do was wrap each leg in white gauze, and every few hours they would unwrap the gauze that stickily clung to the open wound. They would spray a saline solution over the torn flesh, hoping to stave off infection, and then rewrap the wound. The pain was excruciating. Fortunately, they provided a morphine drip with a button that allowed me to inject a dosage into the IV piped into my arm. I was restricted to releasing the narcotic every three to five minutes but it helped keep the pain at bay.

I was desperate for sleep so I could get away from the pain, but I could only manage to fall asleep for short, infrequent naps.

The intensive care unit was busy. I could see the nurses' station through a large window in my room, and because my door was almost always open, I could hear the chatter of doctors, nurses, and visitors throughout the day and night. Occasionally, doctors would bring medical interns in to view my wounds and explain any procedures and surgeries that had been done. It felt strange to have these groups of people gathered around my bed as if I were an exhibit at a museum while I felt like Death was knocking at my door.

After spending a few days together at the hospital, my parents had agreed to split the first two weeks of my recovery. My dad flew back to Massachusetts so my mom could stay for the first week. My mom spent as much time as she could with me in my room, and many friends and coworkers came to visit. Although it felt awkward to have visitors when I was naked under the sheets, hooked up to machines, and unable to care for myself in even the most basic ways, it was heartening to see them and made me wish I was back on the submarine.

On the third day, when I was still heavily doped up on morphine and feeling delirious, a doctor came in the room, making his usual rounds. He stood by the side of my bed, writing his comments on my clipboard. I tried to focus on his face. All the steel and white in the room made me feel dizzy, the walls blending into the floor and ceiling. I fought through the haze to connect with him. I wanted anything but to be stuck in that room and wanted someone to acknowledge that I would someday be somewhere else. "When can I go back to work?" I asked. He hung up his clipboard and pulled a chair over to the side of the bed.

I imagine that this must be one of the most difficult things a doctor has to do - one that keeps them up nights when they're hard at work in medical school, maybe even makes them question whether this is the career for them. But sometimes I wish he could know what he gave me by being so direct and finally telling me what I had been expecting to hear. He looked me straight in the eye and said, "I have some bad news, son. You may never walk again."

As soon as he said those words, I was filled with a level of determination I had not known before. This jolt of realism gave me a brief moment of clarity, and I was filled with a small burst of energy. I was ready to rise to the challenge, determined to defy all odds, knowing that my faith would carry me. I had been looking for hope and promises of getting better, and although I got the opposite, it was what I needed to continue fighting.

***

I was wheeled into surgery several times during that first week as doctors repaired bones, cleaned out infections, and aligned lost nerves in my left arm, which I was still unable to move. A metal rod was inserted in my right femur to hold it in place and help me avoid being put in a body cast - a ragged line of stitches now lined my right hip. The lower right leg then became the main focus. The process was

9

supposed to be a bone graft, then a muscle graft and finally a skin graft that would allow my body to begin the repair and healing process.

I felt weak and helpless during this time, like a doll that was being stitched back together and could do nothing for itself, but soon I had even more reason to strengthen my resolve to stay alive. During this first week in the hospital, a Marine, also stationed in Hawaii, had come in from a similar motorcycle accident. The Marine, whose name I never learned, severed both legs below his knees on his way to work one morning. During that week, he passed away. I needed to stay focused. My life was on the line and I was not ready to go. I had to stay positive, trying to focus on recovering, maybe one day walking again.

When a neurosurgeon from California was called in for special surgery on the ninth day following the accident, I became optimistic. Maybe I would be able to use my legs again. I wanted out of the hospital - I wasn't eating or sleeping and infections were devouring my body. A feeding tube was inserted into my chest so valuable nutrients could be forced into my system. I desperately needed a boost and I just wanted to live.

My instincts told me that the doctor from California was my last resort. If that surgery didn't work, I knew it would be over. That they might have to amputate was a known risk; my situation was so extreme that I became comfortable with the thought before I went into surgery.

They wheeled me into the operating room as they had so many times since I arrived. I was on a gurney and they first sent me to the anesthesiologist to be put under. The oxygen mixture started flowing; I was becoming sedated so I wouldn't feel a thing or have any idea of what was happening during the surgery.

My life was in the hands of God and the medical staff now. I hoped. I prayed. I just wanted to start all over, be back working again.

10

Several hours later, after the surgery, I began to wake up. Things around me looked familiar. I could see this was the observation room where I usually stayed following any operating procedure. I was still groggy since I had just come out of a deep sedation. It was late, around 10 p.m. I could see my right leg wrapped in a plaster cast but could not feel anything yet. I had not been sure what to expect after the operation but something didn't feel right about a plaster cast.

Slowly, the pain started to creep back in.

I reached for my morphine drip and pushed the button. But something was wrong. The pain went from dull to excruciating in no time at all. I felt awful and was starting to get nauseous. "Nurse!" I tried to scream, but it came out squeaky and muted. No one answered. What was happening? I needed help and couldn't find it. Finally a nurse came into the room and asked how I was doing. "I need help. Something's wrong. Why is there so much pain?" My voice was so raspy and weak she could barely understand me. I tried asking what had happened but she only said that I needed to speak with the doctors. "Get my dad, please," I begged. She left to get him and after what seemed like an eternity, my dad, a pulmonary physician of thirty years, came into the room. He had flown to Hawaii for the week to help watch me, his son from a previous marriage, leaving his wife, two kids and job in Massachusetts behind.

I was wheeled back to my room in the trauma intensive care unit, and my dad started making calls. As it turned out, the surgery didn't take. The specialist from California determined that I had a level three infection, something explained to me as practically gangrene, and no graft would set. The odor from the infection was apparent even through the plaster. My leg smelled foul, like old garbage.

I was frustrated, worried and in the worst pain I had ever been in. My leg was horribly infected and the doctors were saying, "We'll take a look at things in the morning." My dad felt the situation was very serious and was concerned that the infection could spread to my heart.

My leg had to be amputated to save my life.

Dr. Ono was the chief orthopedic doctor for the hospital. He was not tall but had a commanding presence. He was considered one of the foremost orthopedic doctors in Hawaii and quickly rose to head of the department at Tripler Army Medical Center. Dr. Ono was the chief surgeon during my arrival at the ER and had overseen my care since the beginning. My dad called him at home and filled him in on the surgery. He convinced Dr. Ono that the amputation was not only necessary but had to be done immediately to save my fading life. I was prepped for surgery for the second time in six hours. Dr. Ono drove in and conducted the intricate surgery himself.

CHAPTER 3
- MY DECISION TO LIVE-

The day following my amputation surgery, I woke up and felt *alive*. I was lying in my hospital bed, having slept until almost noon, and my dad was waiting by the side of my bed. "The nurses came by. All your vital signs are stable," he said. For the first time since the accident, eight days ago, death was not toying with my body. I had lost 90 pounds and was a frail skeleton of my previous 180-pound frame, but I felt strong and somehow knew things were going to be okay. My body had gone through thirteen surgeries since the wreck and I was still hazy from the morphine drip, but I was alive. I felt a great shift take place, a wave of positive energy. I closed my eyes and tried to absorb the moment.

I had been moved out of the intensive care unit into a room in the orthopedic ward. It was quieter here, with only a handful of nurses for the rooms as compared to many nurses at a busy station in the ICU. I was in a private room with my own bathroom here, and had two pink vinyl and wood chairs for visitors. Flowers ringed the room on the floors and the small table, and cards had been put wherever they could fit.

My left leg was in traction, with bolts screwed into the bones of my foot and lower leg, and my right leg was wrapped in heavy bandages almost up to the top of my thigh. Before the surgery, I hadn't been sure how I would feel when I woke up with one leg gone forever. But it wasn't what might be expected - an emotional moment of regret. Instead, my strongest feeling was relief. After feeling like my body had been drifting closer and closer to death for so many days, like all my energy was consumed by the infections wracking my body, I was finally feeling like life was possible again, and it was worth everything. I had seen the state of my right leg when they unwrapped it to clean what was left of it while I was in the ICU, and it looked like it had been through a meat shredder. The chances of keeping it seemed so slim, I felt like I had lost my leg days ago.

Nurses came less frequently now to monitor my progress and care for me - about three or four times a day. They would clean me with a sponge and bucket of water, but since my legs were in traction or bandaged, stitches ran from an inch below my navel to four inches above it, and my right hip was still a line of stitches, there wasn't much that they could clean. I did get my first shave since the accident, though. My beard had grown in spotty and light because my body had been so sick, and it was good to have a clean face.

My catheter had been removed - although I had to awkwardly roll to my side and pee into a bottle if I wanted to use the bathroom by myself - and my feeding tube had been removed. My first meal of solid food since the accident was Thanksgiving dinner - turkey, mashed potatoes, a pureed vegetable, and apple juice. I took only a few small bites, and it hurt to swallow because I had been on a respirating tube during so many surgeries and a feeding tube for so many days, but it felt promising.

After that first moment of relief after waking up in the ward, I had dozed off, and my dad had left the room. When he came back in and sat by the bed again, I woke up. "Nader," he said. He began smoothing the sheets at the edge of my bed. "What happened to us?" Since I had been in the accident and had seen both of my parents again after not seeing them for so long, it had felt like an opportunity to rebuild the old bridges. Conversation still felt awkward, though. "I don't know, Dad."

He leaned back in his chair and glanced around the room, then sat up quickly and looked at me. "Were you drinking that night?" "No, Dad!" He looked away. I finally broke the silence, wanting to share my positive energy I had felt earlier that day. "Dad, I want to go back to work." He looked at my legs. "You have a long way to go." "I know, but it's what I want to do. I want to go back to submarines and the Navy." It felt good to say it. He nodded, and we were silent for a long time. Eventually, I drifted off again.

Later that day, the doctor who had been assigned to me came in the room, and I told him the same thing. I don't know who I was trying to convince more - the world or myself - that returning to the Navy was possible but I felt like I had to say it to everyone I saw. The doctor tried to prepare me for the worst, saying that my recovery would take time and that it was best to focus on small victories, but nothing was discouraging me from returning to what I had loved so much and where I had felt such a great sense of belonging.

It was set in stone for me when I got the support I needed later that day. Commander Mark W. Kenny, the Captain of USS *Birmingham* where I was stationed, visited me that afternoon as he had every day since my accident. He and my other shipmates were my second family, and they had flooded me with cards, flowers and get-well wishes since the time of my accident. When he walked in the room that day, I think he could tell that something was different. I felt invigorated and alive for the first time in a long time. As soon as we had reached the first pause in our conversation about how I was feeling that day, I declared to Commander Kenny, "I want to go back to the boat, sir. I am not finished with my Navy career." Without hesitation he said, "Whatever you need, Nader. We'll support you."

Just like that, without blinking, he was ready to do anything he could to help. It took me years to learn the magnitude of his support. He, along with the shipmates on my boat, would make the choice to operate short-handed while I recovered from the accident in order to give me an opportunity to come back. At the time all I knew was that Mark commanded my boat and what he said was fact for me. He said it was okay, so in my mind it was settled.

Although I was still in great pain and only starting to heal, I finally felt lucky to be alive. I had been given a second chance and realized that from now on, I would see the world differently, almost having it taken from me. I was aware of where I'd been, where I was now, and what I needed to do - I was not only going to live, I was going to have my life back.

My decision, my choice, was to live.

STAGE TWO:
BUILDING CHARACTER

Chapter 4
- A Dream About God -

I was born in 1971 just outside London, England, in a small town called Rochford to parents of Egyptian and Iranian descent. My dad was studying to become a physician and my mom was working as a nurse in the same hospital. They both left home at an early age to find their independence and seek a different life. Finding commonality in the differences from their surrounding environment, my parents married in England and I was the first born of two from their marriage.

We moved to Erie, Pennsylvania, in 1972 to seek new opportunities in America. Nellie was born in June of that year and shortly thereafter we settled in Pittsburgh as my dad found a job that would advance his career. I was just old enough to make friends in Pittsburgh and had started feeling like I belonged when my parents packed up again and moved us to Augusta, Georgia, where my dad had been offered a medical position at the local Veterans Administration hospital.

Augusta was a much harder place to live; we had a harder time fitting in. It was a Southern white town in the 1970s that was still dealing with integration and racial challenges from the previous decades. To people in our community, especially other kids that did not know better, we were foreign with dark skin but were neither black nor white. The environment was a far cry from a cultured city. To make matters more interesting, my dad was a practicing Muslim and my mother was Baha'i. These religions seemed a world away from overwhelmingly homogenous Augusta.

Within a year of moving to Augusta, my dad decided to move into his own apartment. The reasoning explained to Nellie and me at the time was that it was necessary for my dad to focus on his work away from the distractions of home. We saw my dad on a regular basis but the alienation between my parents became apparent, leaving my sister and me to rely more on each other. Our early childhood involved a great deal of emotional stress and, being so young, it was hard to figure out what was happening.

One night I went to bed crying. I was only seven years old and felt like I didn't fit in at home or in the outside world. My parents yelled a lot and I blamed myself, as many children probably do when their parents fight. Earlier that day, as on many others, to escape a fight between my parents I had walked down the street to the edge of the woods where a trail began. A short walk later I came to the fort we had made that I used as an escape to get away. I knew I had left my fire truck at the fort the night before and wanted to play with my favorite toy. When I got there, I saw it and several other of my treasures burned into charred lumps. The air smelled like burnt plastic. The other kids who picked on me often must have known where my stuff was hidden and had decided to have fun at my expense. I ran home, frustrated, alone, and angry.

That night, although I was still upset and was crying into my pillow, I ended up falling into a peaceful sleep. I slipped into a dream, in which I felt like I was waking up from the nightmare that was my real life. I woke up into a much more pleasant world where everyone was happy. I don't remember exactly what happened in the dream - I only remember that it was a long dream, with my parents and sister there - but what I remember clearly was a strong, comforting presence that was somehow responsible for this happy place. A place where my parents didn't fight, where I didn't feel like an outcast. This place felt much more real than the world of taunting and fear I lived every day, and in my dream, I found comfort. A peace came into me that I can only explain today as the first time God touched my life.

I struggled to interpret that dream for years, confused by the presence, wanting that world to be my real world, but left with a comforting feeling that there was something out there greater than I could ever imagine. For years to come, my life was filled with turmoil, an escape to a world that brought me peace gave me a sanctity that I welcomed. I truly believe that God knows our limits far better than we do. Although I felt out of my comfort zone many times, I knew He would catch me if I fell - somehow I knew that there was a reason that things happen.

CHAPTER 5
- MOVING TO CHARLOTTE -

While my dad was living in his apartment in Augusta, my sister and I would visit him each weekend. It was an odd routine that we didn't understand, but my dad wanted us to spend quality time together. As time passed, we were introduced to Jutta, a medical assistant at the hospital, who would help watch us on weekends when my dad was busy. Not long after that, my parents shared the news that they were getting divorced. I can only recall that times were confusing and I am not sure I fully comprehended what was happening at such a young age.

The divorce was long and complicated. Laws in Georgia required my parents to be separated for one year before completing the divorce. After it was finalized, the long process for legal custody began. For Nellie and me, every weekend was a complicated and emotional ordeal of "he said, she said" from our parents. We were caught up in a tug of war that distanced our feelings and created uncertainty and doubt in our family.

One weekend, my dad brought my sister and me to his bedroom in the apartment. He opened his medical bag and said, "I want to show you this. It is a .38-caliber gun. I had to buy it to protect myself." He claimed that our mom was threatening him. That week, when we were back at our mom's house, our mom tried to convince us that a dark Crown Victoria parked outside the house all weekend was a private investigator whom my dad had hired to monitor us. She kept pointing at the curtains in the den saying, "Look outside and let me know if it's still there. Can you see it?"

It felt like it went on forever. Nellie and I were caught up in our family's hell.

This painful custody battle finally ended in 1982, five years after my parents separated. On the final court day, Nellie and I were required to be there with our parents. It was a weekday, so we arrived at the historic Augusta courthouse with our mom. It seemed empty and had the funny smell of a dusty old building. For the first part of the hearing, Nellie and I had to sit outside the courtroom on a long wooden bench. After an hour of waiting, a court secretary escorted us to the judge's chambers. We walked by our parents, both with solemn expressions. Our mom said, "It's okay, kids. Everything will be fine."

The judge was a wrinkled old man with graying hair and a full-length black robe. He offered us water but we shook our heads no. He then said, "Well, we all know why we're here. I'm sure both of you have been going through quite an ordeal. I want to ask you both an important question. If I gave you two the choice, who would you want to live with?" Nellie and I had been told by both of our parents that this day might come and we had been lobbied hard by both for a long time. I had already thought hard about my choice, and I desperately wanted to live with my dad since I was a boy. I believe Nellie felt just as happy with either but wanted to make sure that she and I would be together. That day, in the chambers with the judge, we both said, "We want to live with our dad."

The final announcement came later that afternoon. We were brought back into the courtroom, this time with everyone present. The judge announced to the audience that custody was in fact awarded to my mom. I was shocked. Had he not heard what I said? How could this be possible? Confused and frustrated, I cried and threw temper tantrums when we returned home with my mother. I did not understand what was happening and this emotional roller coaster was hell. Why was this happening? My dad was very disappointed, but, we were able to continue seeing him every other week.

Later that year, my mom told us that we would be going on a vacation during Christmas break to Charlotte, North Carolina. "I've made some new friends there," she said. We arrived in Charlotte at a small townhome and Nellie and I assumed that we were staying at a friend's house. This wasn't surprising, since we could rarely afford even small luxuries and our mom tried to take us places where she could lessen the financial burdens of traveling. The next day, however, our mom surprised us with the announcement that this was going to be our new home. She said that she loved us and that she was afraid we might have resisted coming to Charlotte. She had a new job working as a psychologist for the county in Charlotte and wanted to start a new life away from Augusta. "Charlotte is a better city than Augusta," she insisted. "The people are nice here, the schools are good and we won't have the problems we did in Augusta." Charlotte was supposed to be more integrated and accepting.

My sister and I went along because we had no choice but also because we wanted to make the best of everything. I was almost twelve, which is a confusing enough time of its own, and had started to live in my own world. Nellie retreated deeper into herself while I used my outgoing and rebellious nature to express my pent-up feelings.

In school I became a troublemaker and welcomed confrontation. I was small and a stranger almost wherever I went so I became a magnet for trouble and problems. Furthermore, as we got to know the Charlotte community, we found the same, although subdued, racist overtones that had existed in Augusta. Even in the neighborhood we lived in, older kids taunted and threatened us because of my mom's Iranian descent. After school, I used to run from the bus stop to the townhouse to avoid getting beaten up by the older kids who lingered around after school.

New opportunities opened up for me as I got older. With my mom working full-time and my lack of interest in hanging around the house, I got a job as a paperboy to fill my afternoons. My desire for financial independence motivated me greatly. I worked my routes for three years before my paper, the *Charlotte Post*, was cancelled. I found myself fifteen years old and still hungry for the work environment and greater independence. I worked briefly at the local Wendy's, which was walking distance from my mom's house, then after getting my driver's license and car started working at a local pizza delivery store. Working evenings provided me an escape from the house and a good use of my time. I amassed tips and wages that dramatically helped my financial independence. For the first time, I was able to purchase substantial things on my own such as a stereo, shoes and tickets to movies.

My newfound financial prosperity created more distance between me and my mother and fueled my desire to become even more independent. Things came to a head when my mother, wanting to pull back what I had been trying to take away, began ordering me around. For the Thanksgiving of my junior year in high school, my mom scheduled a small party, mostly her Baha'i friends. During the week prior to the event, my mother ordered me to attend her party and help around the house. My lack of interest in her friends and desire to do something with my own pals turned the discussion into a screaming match.

With my own car, I left in dramatic fashion to go find Jeff and Randy, two friends I knew were out and about. Randy managed to get his hands on a bottle of tequila from his dad's liquor cabinet and we proceeded to do shots with lime chasers, lounging around an outdoor pool. We finished the whole bottle among the three of us. I found myself in rare and unsightly shape. I got sick that night, and my friend drove me home and left me in the driveway of my mom's house, scared that my mother might tell on them. I attempted to go inside the house without disrupting anyone only to create an awful confrontation with my mom. In my drunken stupor, I tried to blame the vomiting on food poisoning but she knew beyond the shadow of a doubt that I had been drinking. The next day, beyond all hope that either of us was doing any good for the other, she asked me to leave the house. Almost happy to finally have the triggering moment to leave home, I packed my bags and left. I believed I would find a way.

I called Jeff to share the news and he mentioned a mutual buddy, Todd, who might be able to take me in. Jeff said that I could stay with his family until I heard from Todd, but that we would have to wait until after Thanksgiving. My feasting dinner of the great American holiday was spent next to a parking lot full of Christmas trees for sale. I dragged trees from the sale lot over to my spot and piled them up to block the wind so I could stay warm through the night. I was filled with pain from my troubling situation with my mother, yet invigorated by my newfound freedom, however frail. Jeff met me out the next day and I spent two nights at his house.

Later that weekend, I got an offer from Todd and his roommate, Charlie, to sublet the living room couch in their small, two-bedroom hole of an apartment for $100 per month. I knew I could afford it with my pizza delivery job while still going to school, so I jumped at the opportunity. Todd had graduated from the same high school I was attending, only nineteen years old himself, and had sympathy for my situation. He was an aspiring police academy applicant who was filling his waiting days working part-time jobs. Charlie was a native West Virginian who found himself without a driver's license following two recent DUIs. I found great comfort among two roommates who had their own troubled situations.

CHAPTER 6
- ARRESTED -

The classroom intercom, an ancient wooden speaker box with gold mesh across the front, buzzed in: "Ms. Garmon, do you have a Mr. Elguindi in your class?" Ms. Garmon paused in grading her papers. "Yes." "Could you please send him to the principal's office?...And tell him to bring his things with him." There was some oohhing from the class and the butterflies in my stomach went haywire.

I gathered my things and walked reluctantly down the hallways of East Mecklenburg High School to the principal's office. As I walked through the administrative door, I was greeted by the assistant principal, an oversized black man who looked like a huge football player twenty years after his career was over. In a deep, intimidating voice he said, "Mr. Elguindi, what trouble have you gotten into?" He pointed behind me. A police officer I had not noticed when I walked in was standing in the back of the room. "Son, I am placing you under arrest," he said, then proceeded to read me my Miranda rights. He pulled out a small laminated piece of paper and uttered some words that hardly registered in my brain my thoughts were spinning out of control.

"According to the law, I have to put these cuffs on you, but if you cooperate, I will take them off when we get to the car, okay?" I was stunned and could not get out even a word. I would have cried if I could have mustered any emotion other than shock.

He drove with me in the back of his police car for the twenty-minute ride to the downtown station. I was then escorted through a series of doors, fingerprinted, and photographed in what seemed like a surreal chain of events. I surrendered my things to an officer and was guided to a holding cell where I waited for what seemed like forever.

An hour passed before I was moved from the cell to the assistant district attorney's office. She motioned toward a straight-backed wooden chair and I sat down across the desk from her. "You have been arrested for trying to cash a forged check," she began. "We pulled information on the check you tried to cash and found out that the checkbook was stolen from a young mother three miles from the bank."

"I got the check from a friend," I stuttered. The truth.

"Bullshit! I think you were desperate for money. Picked up this lady's purse in the park and tried to make out with a few bucks. The signature is a pretty good forgery, so maybe you were working with someone. How am I doing so far?"

I couldn't speak. Just frantically shook my head.

The assistant district attorney built a whole story of me being locked up in the county jail if things progressed. I envisioned all the horrible stories you hear and see about being in a jail cell and feared for my life. "We can work out a deal," she said. "Just tell me the truth." I could not believe what was happening. On the verge of tears, I spilled everything I could about what had happened.

"I was cashing the check for Vincent, the manager of the pizza delivery shop where I work, and one of his friends, Frank." I had few good influences around me; Vincent was someone I looked up to. He accepted me for who I was and even let me hang out with his friends. I knew Vincent was a little questionable, always bringing cocaine around and smoking dope every weekend, but who was I to judge? I was sixteen at the time and living on my own, working forty hours a week and still in high school. Vincent gave me a good job and paid me well enough.

Then one day, Vincent called in a favor.

"He said that he needed my help because he needed the money for the weekend. I had a bad feeling about it, but I didn't ask any questions. Vincent was my manager and my friend. He also promised to take me out to dinner once the check was cashed. Vincent prepped me with what to say if people at the bank started asking me questions."

The assistant district attorney narrowed her eyes, looking skeptical.

"He drove me to the bank, just a few miles away. I walked in with the endorsed check and asked to cash it. The teller was about to give me the money, three hundred dollars, when her manager stepped up and asked to talk to her. I was getting nervous, so after a few minutes, I said, 'Listen, I can do this another time,' and was ready to walk out the door when the manager asked me to step into her office. She asked where I got the check and I told her it came from someone who bumped into my car, just as Vincent had told me. 'I have an old car,' I told her. 'It's a '78 Chevy and not worth much. Someone hit me when I slowed down on the railroad tracks. Bothering with the police and insurance was too much trouble, so she gave me the check to cover the cost of damages.' The bank manager believed me."

I shifted uncomfortably in my chair. This was hell. Everything I said, the assistant district attorney double-checked on the notes she had been given.

"But then the police arrived. The manager told them about my story and then I went into a private office in the bank. Just the police and me. They asked all the same questions again, and I had to write a detailed account of the story exactly as I had told it to the manager. I did and they were happy for the time being. Two weeks later, I was being called out of Ms. Garmon's classroom."

"That's it?"

"That's it."

"What are Vincent's and Frank's last names?" she asked, looking down at her notes.

When I gave her their full names, her head flew up, and she looked straight at me. "Do you know how thick my file is on this guy? He is wanted for more crimes than I have time to deal with. His dad is a high-ranking government official and every time his name comes up, I have to wash everything clean. Not one arrest. It can't happen."

"But that's the truth."

"For what it's worth, I believe you," she said. "But you're on your own."

I was alone. Again.

I spent the night in the jail cell before someone came to pick me up. "You're being bailed out," the sheriff said. I gathered my things and scurried quickly out of the jail, curious as to who was freeing me. As I walked through the long hallway I could see my mother standing in the lobby. She started berating me with questions before we left the building. "What happened? What did you do?" I tried to explain as best I could, but my mother and I still had a fragile relationship. Still, I was indebted to her for bailing me out. She drove me back to my apartment and I promised to keep her informed as things developed. Going back to school was no easy thing either but I decided it was the best thing to do. The court hearing was a few weeks away and I had no idea what was going to happen.

At that time, my dad was living in Saudi Arabia with his new family. He had moved there a few years earlier, citing the bitter divorce and custody battle as reasons he went to live abroad. He was a well-respected pulmonary physician of Egyptian descent, and Saudi Arabia was known for paying doctors handsomely. My dad heard about the trouble I got into through my sister and called me to find out what happened. The conversation was short, and at the end he said, "I'm coming to visit. I'll be there next week."

During the visit, he wanted to hear about my deteriorating relationship with my mother and the trouble I had gotten into with the forged check. He promised to help and even started sending the $500 alimony checks directly to me to help cover my expenses. He also said, "I want you out of the apartment-sharing situation with Todd and Charlie. You need to get away from the drugs." I tried to protest that I was not part of the drugs but could see that leaving that situation was a good idea. He also hired a criminal lawyer in Charlotte to help me with the hearing.

I prayed like I had never prayed before. I was in a deep valley and needed a ray of sunlight. I made a promise to God that night: "If I get out of this situation, I promise to improve everything. I won't let You down. Please help," I begged.

Despite my faith and continued prayers to God, there were days when I questioned everything. I was now living in a tiny apartment on my own and didn't have roommates to check on me or for companionship. I recall one Friday night when I was in the kitchen of my dark apartment, the florescent light flickering and softly buzzing. With nothing to do and little money to do anything with, I was making boxed macaroni and cheese and ramen noodles for dinner. I opened the drawer to find a knife to open the box and picked one out from the set. I sat there with the knife in my hand, regretting the events that had taken place and dreading the sentencing that would ultimately come. "Wouldn't it be nice to be in a better place?" I thought. It was a blessing that I was too weak to do anything drastic.

***

A few days later, I got a call from my lawyer. "I worked out a deal with the district attorney. You'll get one year of probation, and if everything goes well, a subsequent expungement, which will remove this event from your record." I was ecstatic about not having to go to jail and thanked God. We went to court the following week and I accepted the terms in front of the judge and district attorney.

For the next year, I visited my appointed probation officer monthly beginning in May of my junior year in high school. She was supportive and did not judge me based on my actions - only forward progress. Her focus was on my employment and grades in school. I was now seventeen years old, and if I followed her program, I would be finished with probation before I graduated high school. I had an opportunity to get out, so I set my sights on walking the straight line until then. I had made a promise and I intended to keep it.

With renewed focus, my own apartment, and a mission to clean up my act, I started looking for a new job. My neighbor, Jon, mentioned an opening at the hospital where he was working, Charlotte Memorial Hospital. The position was in the ER, checking in patients during the triage process. For a high school kid, the pay was very good, around $9 per hour, with regular shift work and overtime for anything over forty hours a week. Jon's referral proved fruitful and I was hired by Ms. Barbaree, the supervisor for the hospital business office. With school soon ending for summer break, I wanted to work as many hours as possible just to keep my mind off other things. Being young, with so much energy, I was able to put in between fifty and sixty hours each week during summer break. I also found another part-time job at a new pizza place called PDQ a few miles away, where I was able to put my previously learned skills to good use during the peak weekend nights. My social life was nonexistent but I was on a mission. Working was a good outlet for me.

My senior year of high school started in August, and I welcomed it with vigor. I had saved several thousand dollars working two jobs during the summer and had stayed clear of any issues the entire time. Things were working well with my probation officer. During the week, I spent long hours studying for class and didn't miss a day of school, unlike my junior year of regular skipping. My grades turned around from a C average to a 4.0 my senior year. Things were starting to go well and I had my sights set on graduating. One year earlier I had been in the pits, considering dropping out, and now I had found new motivation. My life was finally working out.

By May 1989 I was on track to graduate high school. I had completed my probationary duties and had selected Appalachian State University as my college. I planned to continuing working through the summer, saving money, then pack my bags and say goodbye to the apartment complex I had called home for two years. I eagerly awaited my future - a chance to start anew.

CHAPTER 7
- COLLEGE -

Everything I owned and was interested in taking with me to college fit into my small Ford Tempo. The trunk and backseat full, I traveled up Highway 421, a four-lane road that carried me up into the mountains. Appalachian State University sat inside a valley at the top of the mountains next to a small western North Carolina town called Boone. Even with our small campus of 11,000 students, the town population doubled when school began each August. As a freshman, I had been directed to show up a week early for orientation. My little car struggled to get up the windy mountain roads, weighed down as it was. I could see the town over the crest of the last hill with signs on every corner saying something about Appalachian State University. I followed my map to the Cone Building, my freshman dorm hall, as directed by the welcoming packet I had received in the mail.

I pulled my car into a small parking lot that could not have fit ten cars. Dozens of other freshmen were emptying their cars into the all-male Cone dorm building. Some were escorted there by parents or friends and others were just unloading on their own. The whole dorm was filled with others just like me venturing off to college, many on their own for the first time. I carried my first handful of bags to the fourth floor, room 421, as instructed. I opened the door and a tall, pale, dark-haired guy was lying on one of the beds reading a book. "Hi, I'm Mike. You must be Nader?" he said. My newfound roommate was a quiet, confident, 6'1" guy from Atlanta, Georgia, with a strong handshake. He offered to help me unload and I welcomed the assistance. I had made my first new friend at college and was spell-bound by my new environment. I felt at home and realized I would be here for the next four years, which seemed like an eternity.

Mike turned out to be the perfect roommate. He was calm, easygoing, attended church regularly and encouraged me when I needed it. We joined the same orientation class and spent the first week hanging together for meals and playing sports around campus, including basketball and tennis. Mike was intelligent and athletic, which kept me motivated and fueled my competitive nature.

After the first few weeks, Mike asked me to join him for fraternity rush. I was unfamiliar with the process and my only knowledge of fraternities was through a few movies I had seen, including *Animal House* with John Belushi. Mike told me that it would be a great way to meet people and socialize. He had done some studying up and had picked three fraternities he wanted to check out. I was talked into coming more because I had nothing to do than because I had any real interest in joining a fraternity.

During one of the rush events, I met a great group of guys who were hungry to be a bigger chapter - the Delta Chi Fraternity. One particular member, John, and I hit it off and I found myself wanting to be part of this group. Mike and I discussed the options and agreed to apply for Delta Chi. Within weeks, I found myself cast into a group of new friends from all kinds of diverse backgrounds and making my way to classes each week, learning new things and meeting interesting new classmates and teachers.

On weekends I would go back to Charlotte so that I could work at the hospital and make a few bucks. I didn't have an apartment in Charlotte anymore, but I did end up developing a friendship with a hallmate in my dorm who was also from Charlotte, Brian Wallace. Brian was a complete contrast from me but he needed a ride home on weekends and his parents let me stay at their house. His father was a Presbyterian minister and his mother, Sissy, was a working mother who had raised three boys. Brian was the middle child and grew up in a cozy and comfortable atmosphere. He was athletic and succeeded socially in high school, becoming class president his senior year. Although he struggled academically, he found ways to make things work by focusing on other areas. In college, he joined the campus a cappella group as well as Sigma Phi Epsilon, one of the largest and most popular fraternities at school.

We went home at least once a month because I needed the money working part-time at the ER and Brian liked having a cheap and easy way to do his laundry. His family was very welcoming to me and I started to go to their church, where his father, Reverend Robert M. Wallace, was head pastor. Reverend Wallace also became a confidant for me when I raised questions about God and Christianity. During the holidays, the Wallace family asked me to stay with them, so I enjoyed Thanksgiving and some of the school breaks with them. They provided support and encouragement for the voids left in my life. I was on my own without even my probation officer to keep me straight, yet I felt empowered with a determination to succeed.

For part of the Christmas holiday during freshman year, my dad asked me to come visit him in Springfield, Massachusetts, where he now lived with his family. I made the twelve-hour road trip up I-95 one weekend after spending a few days in Charlotte working part-time and hanging out with the Wallaces. I enjoyed driving since it gave me some time to free my mind and listen to the music I enjoyed. There was still a big part of me that was intimidated by the world and all the successful people I encountered. I used to think about what made one person so confident and successful and another so challenged by everyday encounters. I was venturing into uncharted territory in my life and while there was excitement at my second change, I was often engulfed by the fear of losing it all again.

I crossed the Massachusetts border and took the first exit into the suburban neighborhood of Longmeadow, south of Springfield. A few miles later, I turned right onto my dad's street and parked in front of his four-bedroom, two-story brick house. There were small snow drifts on the sides of the streets and around the house from the winter season - it looked like a holiday postcard from New England. I grabbed my bags from the back seat and went up to the door, ready to wind down after a long drive up the Eastern seaboard. The house was a well-furnished, upper-middle-class one, and my dad was proud of it, having become a well-respected physician for BlueCross BlueShield of Massachusetts.

My dad welcomed me in the front hallway with a hug and greeting as he always did. I could hear Jutta in the kitchen preparing dinner for the evening and their two kids, Laila and Sharif, chattering and playing in the living room down the hall. Laila was their older child and my half-sister, eleven years younger than me. Sharif, my half-brother, was only three years old at the time, born just before they moved to Springfield.

"It's good to see you, Nader," my dad said, putting his hand on my shoulder. "But we need to discuss the progress of your first year of school. We'll meet in my study downstairs after dinner." A familiar feeling of dread soured my stomach - another time I would have to try to live up my father's expectations - but I tried to put it aside. "Okay, Dad." "Good then. You're in the spare room next to Nellie."

I went upstairs to unload my bags and say hi to my sister. After I left home in Charlotte, she had given up living with our mom and had chosen to move in with Dad, opting to finish her last two years of high school in Springfield. My mom was left to live alone with her work back in Charlotte. Nellie kept up with her, but I was not yet at the mental point of rebuilding a relationship with my mom, in spite of what she had done to help me.

Dinner at the Elguindi house was usually a formal occasion. My father insisted on homemade meals with everyone eating together at the table. Tonight's dinner was held in the dining room instead of at the table in the kitchen, no doubt to celebrate my arrival for Christmas. My dad liked using the nice china and the dining room, and he would choose it on any occasion that seemed appropriate. Jutta had become a phenomenal cook, preparing complex four- and five-course meals that usually included a casserole and almost always a dessert. She had a knack for making cheesecakes, which was my favorite after-dinner dessert.

After dinner my dad watched the news, always choosing ABC *Nightly News* with Peter Jennings. It seemed like a staple in my dad's house - Walter Cronkite when I was growing up and then Peter Jennings after Cronkite retired. At 6 p.m. he issued fierce shushes to the kids, then Jutta would chime in, hurrying the children to other rooms so my dad could focus on the news.

Later that evening, after Sharif was tucked into bed and the house had quieted down, I walked downstairs to the small corner room in the basement that was my dad's office. He sat on a red leather chair behind a large mahogany desk, his impressive certificates peppering the walls. I sat down in a chair across from him.

"How were your grades this semester?" my dad asked.
"Pretty good, I think. Four As and one A-minus. I made the Dean's List."
"I think you can improve," my dad said, his leather chair creaking as he leaned back into it.

I was shocked and had no idea how to respond. I was proud of my first year's academic accomplishment, especially for my good grade in Calculus II, which was taught by a professor who was known throughout the campus as being the school hard-ass. Over half of his students opted for incompletes rather than try to survive in his miserable world of equations.

"You're not focusing enough. If you want me to continue supporting you, I need you to improve. I want your grades to get better and you need to stop doing drugs."
"Drugs? I don't do drugs!"

"You're in a fraternity, and everyone knows that people in fraternities do drugs, smoke pot, and get drunk. I think being in a fraternity is too much of a distraction for you. Do you want to end up in jail again?"

That pushed me over the edge. I was so proud of how much I had accomplished and my dad had just beat me back down as low as I had felt when I was sent to jail. In hindsight, I know he was looking after my best interests, but I got frustrated and started yelling. "I don't need you or your money. Fuck off!" I ran upstairs to pack my things and jumped into my car, speeding out of Springfield, skipping Christmas and the rest of my holiday vacation at Dad's.

I was alone. Again.

I resumed school in January ready to take on a new semester at college, where I was starting to find some success. I decided to focus on a business marketing degree and packed my course load to get things done quickly. I started visiting Charlotte more frequently, trying to make as much income as possible through my part-time employment at the ER. My father wrote me after a couple of months trying to ask what was the matter with me but I ignored his comments and never replied. I was determined to do things on my own.

Fatigue was starting to set in and my school debt was building up. By the end of my freshman year I had amassed almost $2,000 in credit card debt. I could not qualify for school loans because of my financial situation and only qualified for limited grants and scholarships. I was able to pick up a $250 Dean's List scholarship and a $500 grant for my achievements in science, but it wasn't enough.

In May of that freshman year, Thad, a classmate from my physics class, invited me to a Navy recruiting event on campus. Two naval officers came to our school for the day to introduce people to their nuclear engineering program. I laughed at the thought but Thad was genuinely interested and talked me into going. The men were very nice and used the enticing tagline of "seeing the world" combined with a free tour of a top-secret submarine base in Kings Bay, Georgia. The tour was scheduled for June after classes were out, so Thad and I jumped at the opportunity to milk a free vacation.

The Navy flew us down to Kings Bay on a Friday afternoon and we were escorted to our own Bachelor Officers' Quarters (BOQ) rooms on base. That afternoon, we were joined by ten other underclassmen interested in learning more about what the Navy had to offer. The weekend started off with a tour of the base and its amenities. Kings Bay was one of the newest and most sophisticated naval bases in the country. The tour and detail was fascinating. I had never been introduced to anything like it. Saving the best for last, they then took us on a tour of the USS *Tennessee*, docked pier-side in a channel leading to the Atlantic Ocean. The submarine was a complex and intricate engineering phenomenon. "The nuclear reactor generates enough power to carry a small city," said the tour guide, a man dressed in a khaki uniform. "Once you become qualified, you can drive the submarine as Officer of the Deck. And one day, you can even captain your own sub!"

I was hooked.

Later that month, we were taken to Raleigh, North Carolina, where the Navy recruiting office was headquartered for our state. They talked about what our obligation would be, including a five-year commitment following graduation. We would be offered a $15,000 per year scholarship for a maximum of two years. I quickly realized that this amount would cover all my costs and expenses.

The only catch was that I would have to pass the naval reactor exam in Washington, D.C. The Navy recruiters informed me that this would be a purely academic test for which I would be given two months to study. I would then be flown to D.C. to take the tests. If I passed, I was accepted. I would be required to change my degree to a science or engineering degree and I had to graduate two years from the acceptance of my Navy commitment. Being at the end of only my freshman year, I would have to graduate college in three years! It seemed incomprehensible but waiting another year would bankrupt me for sure.

I was hungry for success and financial freedom. This opportunity seemed too good to be true, so I made some calls and started researching the likelihood. After speaking with my professors and the dean, I found out I could make it work by cramming eighteen hours into each semester and taking classes during summer school. Without the obligation to work every weekend, I felt that it was possible. I called the Raleigh office and informed them I wanted to do it. I would take the exam and make the commitment.

The night before I was to fly to D.C., I drove from Boone to Charlotte and stayed with the Wallaces. I shared my plans with them and they encouraged me and prayed for me. In D.C., I and about eleven other applicants were escorted to a hotel room near Pentagon City - we were all there hoping to find our way into the Navy. The officers escorting us gave us one last rundown of how things were going to happen, and then we were guided across the street into a dreary-looking government building - the Bureau. Inside was what you might expect to see in a dingy old courthouse. Stone floors and walls decorated only with a series of photos of men in gray suits, one of whom I recognized as the president of the United States.

We were split into groups and took clanky elevators to the third floor, where we waited in a small lobby until our names were called, one by one. Finally it was my turn. "Mr. Elguindi? This way, please." I was escorted by a woman to a small room around the corner that had a large blackboard on one side and two men standing against the opposite wall. The room resembled a college classroom but had a formal feeling that was far from school. The two men greeted me coldly and asked me to sit next to the blackboard. The interview began.

For over an hour they asked me questions, quizzing my knowledge of engineering on several levels. I had been given a study guide by the recruiters in Raleigh and had spent the better part of my summer memorizing what I needed to. I felt comfortable with the first exam and the men informed me that I now was supposed to go to the next room. I walked down the hall as directed and opened another door. This room was similar to the first but had only one person, a much younger man than the two before.

I struggled during the second exam and fought through tougher questions that were much more subjective than I had expected. After another hour passed, I was told to go out and wait in the lobby until further instruction. We had been told from the beginning that most Naval Reactor exams require two tests. A third is offered if there is doubt as to the ability of the student or for further clarification. After a few minutes, the lady who had come to me before asked me to follow her again. I was offered a third test and my nervousness was showing. Luckily, the third exam was on chemistry and thermodynamics - a course I had just taken the previous semester. I whizzed through the questions flawlessly and gained a new sense of confidence. Back in the lobby again, I found myself waiting for the last part of the test. It was an interview with Admiral DeMars, the head of Naval Reactors for the entire Navy.

The Navy nuclear program was founded by Admiral Hyman G. Rickover in the late 1940s. He was a bright and temperamental Navy officer who found himself leading the nuclear cause in America following World War II. He created a system of detail and perfection that rivaled every program in the world. In almost fifty years of operation, the Navy had not had a single nuclear incident or problem. He was a small man who had a legendary reputation for demolishing people's egos. Traditionally, the last interview was to be one of intimidation to determine if a candidate had the backbone to survive in the nuclear Navy, which could involve being at sea for six months at a time.

45

Admiral DeMars was an aging man who had served for over thirty years in the Navy. He sat behind a large oak desk, looking down as if studying something as I walked in.

"Sit down," he said without looking up or shaking my hand. A few moments passed - it felt like an eternity.

"Why did you choose ASU?" he asked.

I paused at the question, then answered, "Because it's a good school," as the best response I could come up with.

"There are many good schools in North Carolina. NC State, Duke, Carolina, Wake Forest. Couldn't you pick a better school? Why should I accept someone from a podunk mountain college?"

I had worked so hard to get where I was, but when he asked that question, I knew that the reason I had gone to Appalachian was because I couldn't get accepted anywhere else. My response had to be strong, though. I mustered everything I had and blurted out a squeaky statement with obvious emotion: "ASU is a great school. It has a better professor to student ratio than all those schools and is certainly as capable." I could not believe that all I was able to dig up in my flurrying head was something about the student to professor ratio. What was I thinking?

He then expressed to me what I felt was rejection in no uncertain terms: "Get out of my office. The interview is finished."

I tried to say something but was left speechless. I turned and walked out of his office, furious that things had ended so badly. If that was the trial of character and strength, I knew it was over. I was instructed by a small elderly lady outside the admiral's office to wait in the sitting room to my left. It was a large, stately room with high ceilings and a long, dark, wood conference table. Red leather chairs surrounded the table and the walls were decorated with art complementary to the intimidating atmosphere. I sat for thirty minutes with nothing to do but second-guess my efforts and resulting failure.

The door creaked open and a woman stepped into the room, a single manila folder in her hands. I stood. "Mr. Elguindi?" I nodded. "Congratulations, you have been accepted into the Navy Nuclear Engineering Program. Please take this file downstairs to complete your paperwork."

I stood motionless.

I was accepted. It rang through my head and I had to ask her twice just to confirm that it was true. Downstairs I was greeted by the two officers from Raleigh who had brought me to D.C. They already knew I had been accepted and congratulated me before escorting me across the street to the bar in the hotel where we were staying. The other men from our group were there as well and I immediately went over to Thad. He had been accepted earlier and I was the last of our bunch.

My future was set.

The Navy had solved my financial woes and given me a new lease on life. My next seven years were locked in and I had a new mission to fulfill. I was on my way to becoming a naval officer. God had answered my prayers and now it was my turn to complete my obligation.

CHAPTER 8
- MY NAVY CAREER -

College graduation day meant a great deal more to me than I imagine it meant to my classmates. Four years earlier, I had been facing a judge in Charlotte and saw only a gray, dismal future. Now, I had finished college in three years with a respectable 3.6 average and was looking forward to a career as an officer in the United States Navy. I was incredibly proud of the opportunity to serve my country and was relieved that I had a positive future.

In college, Brian Wallace had become one of my best friends during those weekend road trips to Charlotte. His family treated me like one of their own, and I invited all of them to my graduation. My mom and I had found mutual terms of sorts and she came that day as well. I was just another student among thousands who graduated from ASU in 1992, but for me it was a small miracle.

I had received my formal orders from the Navy a few months earlier. They gave me six days following graduation to report to Newport Naval Station in Rhode Island for Officer Candidate School (OCS). I used the time to pack my things and say my goodbyes. That Saturday I woke early, eager for my journey, and made the trip up the Eastern seaboard for the first time since my freshman year. This time I drove right past the Hartford interchange and continued on I-95 to Rhode Island. I found the naval station buried on the north side of the small whaling town of Newport. It was early June and the days were long, so the sun had just set as I pulled into base. My instructions indicated that I was to report to King Hall and, after a few directions from helpful people, I found myself just outside a four story, U-shaped brick building that looked relatively nondescript among a cluster of similar buildings.

I parked my white Ford Tempo in front of the building and popped my trunk to get my bags out. The Navy had given me specific instructions about what to bring and how much storage was allowed, but, unlike others, I was traveling with my lifetime of belongings, so my car was relatively full. As I was walking to the trunk to grab my bags, a slender black man in uniform came storming out of the front door. I turned to him just as he started yelling. "What the hell are you doing, plebe? Drop those bags. Get on the deck. Get your ass inside King Hall. Do as I say. Get down, now!"

I spent the next four hours getting yelled at and screamed at by senior classmen while I and the other new candidates were ordered to do everything from seemingly endless rounds of push-ups to running in circles.

Hell Week had just begun. This is when students train for a solid five days and five nights with a minimum amount of sleep. Hell Week begins on Sunday and ends on Friday. During this time, trainees face continuous training evolutions. They wake up before dawn and get breaks only for meals. The rigorous regiment of Hell Week is designed to humble every officer candidate and train everyone to work together as a team. In addition, it emphasizes the importance of critical decision-making in the face of fatigue.

The week was a rigorous regimen of physical exercise and various military discipline-training exercises and marches. They shaved our heads and dressed us in hideous moss-colored jumpsuits so that we would all look the same. "Uniform is part of your discipline!" they screamed out.

Following the end of Hell Week, we were officially inducted as officer candidates and informed that we had sixteen more weeks to complete our training. OCS is a general training and initiation that everyone not part of the Naval Academy or ROTC is required to do to get a commission in the Navy. The terminology "officer candidate" was used to identify all of us in training to become commissioned officers. Some of the officer candidates were in program tracks to become nuclear engineers, or "nukes," like me, and others were everything from general line officers who would fulfill admin duties to civil engineers who would help with building and construction projects for the Navy. As the weeks at OCS progressed, we were given more freedoms, including occasionally leaving base on the weekends.

Newport was a beautiful town with plenty of young, attractive people spending their summers along the shore and partying out on the docks at night. Boston was only a short one-hour drive up the coast. I found a small rat pack of friends, four of us, who spent time together on the weekends. Paul, my roommate at OCS, was a small, dark-haired kid from Manhattan. John Stearn was a Southern boy at heart, having grown up in Virginia and recently graduated from Virginia Tech. Chris was Midwestern through and through. He was from Montana and had gone to school at Kansas University. All of us complemented each other well, and we tore up the town on weekends and partied in Boston when we could.

The time in Newport flew by and, before I knew it, graduation and commissioning day was around the corner. The commissioning ceremony of an officer candidate in the military is an important and distinguished honor. For me, it was the symbolic completion of my long journey.

U.S. Code requires the administration of the Oath of Office to be conducted by a commissioned officer of the armed forces, either active or retired, and an officer candidate can choose to have a family member or close friend who is a commissioned officer in this role. My Uncle Tom was a retired Army officer. He had started his military career by serving two tours in Vietnam and completed a twenty-four-year career, retiring as an infantry officer who made it to the rank of major after quickly ascending through the enlisted ranks and getting his college degree while working full-time. I had confided in Tom when I was considering whether to join the Navy and he had provided experience and guidance that confirmed my decision to be a part of the military.

Having my Uncle Tom commission me made the moment that much more special and memorable. To this day, I still proudly hang the picture of me in my white uniform holding my right hand up, swearing to defend our country while my uncle, in his highly decorated Army green uniform, has me recite the Oath of Office.

> *"I, Nader Elguindi, do solemnly swear that I will support and defend the Constitution of the United States against all enemies, foreign and domestic; that I will bear true faith and allegiance to the same; that I take this obligation freely, without any mental reservation or purpose of evasion; and that I will well and faithfully discharge the duties of the office on which I am about to enter. So help me God."*

Following OCS, all nuclear engineering officers go through two more schools of training. The first was Nuclear Power School (NPS) at Orlando Naval Base, Florida. The second was prototype school, which for me was in Charleston, South Carolina.

NPS was our first exposure to secret material and the true flavor of the exciting world of submarines. As with the start of every transfer or order change to a new base, we had to begin with check-ins. The check-in steps were to assure we had everything in order prior to starting our duties. One critical step in that process was our secret clearance. As submariners, secret clearance was necessary for all training and SCI (Special Compartmentalized Information) clearance for all operational missions. SCI is one of the highest clearances in the military, being the next level above Top Secret, and is taken very seriously. All of our clearance investigations were conducted by the Naval Investigative Service (NIS). The investigations involved in-depth background searches and included interviewing the people we had known. For me, that was everything from phone searches to meeting with teachers and fraternity brothers back at ASU. No stone was left unturned.

When my turn came around to getting my clearance, I was informed it was still pending and had not come through yet. Since it was still in progress, I was held back in class. The next class was scheduled in two months, so I had to wait, working a temporary job at an administrative office, until everything was completed in order for me to gain my clearance.

Finally, I got the call from NIS saying that they required a meeting with me. I went to the NIS facility at the pre-set time and date in uniform, anxious to get my clearance. The NIS officer informed me that this was a formal interview and it would be recorded. He was a large blond man in a blue suit and tie. Although he was friendly towards me, the atmosphere created a certain amount of tension. He asked me several questions about my past, sometimes asking the same question twice in different ways, trying to catch me changing my answer. I had to explain the fact that I did occasionally drink in high school and reiterate there were a few instances where I smoked marijuana. Everything went well until he slid a photocopied piece of paper across the table. "What is this?" he asked. I read it and was brought right back to that day in high school when I was in the principal's office and a policeman read me that very warrant for my arrest.

It hit me - this might be the end. I wasn't going to get my clearance.

"I was arrested in high school," I stated, but that was not enough. He wanted all the details - everything. I told him the story that had both haunted and motivated me since I was seventeen. After I had finished the story, he was silent a moment and simply stared at me. I could hear every creak of my chair. Finally, he asked the question I was dreading: "Why was this not noted on your application?" I explained that I thought the record had been expunged. "I did not want to disclose information that was unnecessary or might be inconsistent with my records. I was a juvenile when it happened and thought it had been completely erased." The other half of the story was obvious; I had thought it would threaten my future to put that I had a record on my application. I was moving on and I did not want my past holding me back.

The funny thing, though, is that the past never leaves us. The past becomes part of the soil we stand on. Some of it's good, some of it isn't, but we can't do anything about it once it has happened. That seems like such a simple thing, but it took me years to figure that out. At that time in my life, I was so eager to start a good path that I envisioned everything happening before me as chalk on a blackboard that I could just erase away.

I went home that day and prayed. It was out of my hands and the only thing ringing in my head was the NIS officer's last comment: "Thank you for your cooperation. We'll be in touch."

Two weeks later, while I was working at the administrative office, I received a call from NIS. "Your clearance has come through. Official papers indicating you are cleared for NPS will be in the mail." I informed my supervising officer and was directed to prepare for the NPS class starting in January. I was on my way, once again.

***

Nuclear Power School is a six-month program that is equivalent to earning a Master's degree in nuclear engineering. There were approximately twenty classes we took during that period, each one ending in a final exam. The courses were all advanced, including such subjects as hydrodynamics and nuclear chemistry. Class was held from 0730 until 1730: 5:30 p.m. in military time. We were required to log an additional thirty to forty hours of study time per week based on our grades and since everything was classified secret, all material had to remain within the facility. On average, we spent anywhere from seventy to eighty hours each week training and studying for this school. It was by far the hardest academic program I have participated in and at that time was ranked as the second most difficult academic program in the country behind Harvard by *U.S. News & World Report*. Following the six-month program we had to pass one comprehensive exam that incorporated sections from each of the twenty classes we took. This ultimate final exam lasted eight hours.

I ended up in the bottom half of my class, but since it was pass or fail, I completed everything as satisfactory for graduation. The company I was in included graduates from Harvard, MIT, Cal Berkeley, Stanford and one friend who was valedictorian at Yale. Among such distinguished classmen, I felt proud even graduating such a rigorous academic program. Another small miracle, and I still couldn't believe my education came from the mountains of Appalachia. The dream had started to take form and my future was becoming certain.

For the first time, I started to envision my life revolving around the military. I met senior officers along the way and started to appreciate and welcome the idea of family that the Navy created. I wanted to become a "lifer," as they call it. Earlier that year, I had met a beautiful young redhead named Sandi who was working at the Orlando base MWR office. We hit it off immediately and I fell head over heels in our sprouting relationship. In addition, her father was a captain in the Navy, serving as base commander for the Orlando Naval Base. Sandi was intimately familiar with the Navy life, having grown up in the military.

Following Nuclear Power School graduation we were all allowed to pick any submarine base we wanted to be stationed once the upcoming Prototype and Sub School training were complete. Since there were six sub bases in the country, we could get fairly close to any area we wanted. A couple of my friends were encouraging me to pick Hawaii, since that was the most exotic location. The Navy also tried to encourage the single guys to go there since it was more cost-effective to ship singles, as well as other reasons. Since my involvement with Sandi had started to influence decisions I was making, when the time came around to pick our permanent duty station, I told my recruiter I wanted to go to Norfolk, Virginia. The recruiters have to juggle many people and assignments, so we were told that it would be a few months before we knew our official station.

The next stop in my training was Nuclear Prototype School in Charleston, South Carolina. There were three Prototype schools across the country, one in upstate New York and the other in Idaho, but I choose Charleston to be close to Sandi and because I loved the warm beaches and historic aspect of the city. Prototype was the operational complement to what Nuclear Power School in Orlando provided. Where we had mostly studied books and theory in Orlando, at Prototype we practiced what we learned on an old, decommissioned submarine that was tied to the docks. Prototype School was also six months long, and, unlike the daily routine of Power School, we had to work shifts in Charleston. Since the reactor was in operation twenty-four hours a day and they were trying to simulate what a working environment is like at sea, we worked in twelve-hour increments for blocks of days. With supporting class work to complement the operational practice, we often spent sixteen to twenty hours on base during duty days. Every four days or so, we would get a break and I would use the time to visit Sandi in Florida.

One of my shipmates had a fairly new motorcycle, a black Kawasaki Ninja ZX-6, which his father had given him for college graduation. After learning he was not much of a rider, he sold me the motorcycle and it became my primary means of transportation. I used to zip down the coastline from Charleston to Orlando on my bike, barely stopping along the way. Two tanks of gas and six hours later, I would arrive in sunny Orlando. Sandi and I spent a great deal of time together and some weekends she would visit me in Charleston.

After a few months of back and forth travel, our relationship started to feel strained, and Sandi had second thoughts about being part of the Navy during her adult life. Things finally came to an end during one of her visits to Charleston. I was devastated and depressed for weeks but with working eighty or more hours a week, I didn't have time to give it too much thought. One afternoon, while on base in

Charleston, I used my break to call the Navy recruiter in charge of my orders. With no major tie holding me to the East Coast, I mentioned that my situation has changed and asked him whether Hawaii was still available. He said he would see what he could do but no promises. My assignment came in just a few weeks before we completed Prototype. I was set to report to the USS *Birmingham*, stationed in Pearl Harbor.

I was going to Hawaii.

***

The final stage in my submarine schooling took place in cold and dreary New London, Connecticut. Groton Naval Base was a small, dark base that housed the only sub school in the country. Every officer and enlisted man was required to learn the basic operations of a submarine including fire-fighting, damage control and basic operational knowledge. I was there during the winter of 1993, so we enjoyed good skiing on the weekends. After four months of the coldest and snowiest winter I had seen, I was more than ready for tropical Hawaii.

Prior to my move to Hawaii, I was given thirty days of vacation to report to my new duty station. It was considered a final reward for two years of hard training as well as time to wrap up whatever little items were necessary before we went away for the next three years. My goodbyes were short and sweet, so I spent most of my time off fulfilling a lifelong goal: traveling across the country in a Jeep. I drove from the East Coast across the northern states along Highway I-70. In Indiana, I cut south and crossed the Mississippi through St. Louis, visiting the Gateway Arch, the "gateway to the west." Most of my trip, however, was spent in Colorado, which I still consider one of the most beautiful states in America. While in Colorado, I climbed Pike's Peak, a 14,000-foot mountain deep inside the Rockies. Pike's Peak is a symbol of American heights and climbing it symbolized my personal journey. After reaching the summit, I was winded beyond belief but managed to get a photo of myself standing on the top of the mountain.

Later, during that trip, I stopped along the Grand Canyon, another place I had always dreamed of visiting. The grandeur of nature left me in awe. At one of the stores, I found a t-shirt that has a unique statement on it that has stayed with me:

> *"Success is to be measured not so much by the position that one has reached in life as by the obstacles which he has overcome"* - *Booker T. Washington*.

I adopted that phrase as my own and felt a sense of peace overcome me that trip. God helped me along this road and journey, and I sensed my destiny ahead. The last leg of my vacation was a flight from Los Angeles to Hawaii after dropping my car off at the docks of Long Beach for its boat trip across the Pacific.

CHAPTER 9
- ARRIVING ON THE USS *BIRMINGHAM* -

The flight from Los Angeles to Honolulu was six hours long and I was so anxious my skin was about to crawl around on its own. This was my first visit to Hawaii and I was moving to a land not only 6,000 miles from home but to a culture that was far from anything I had ever experienced. The flight captain said over the speaker, "Ladies and gentlemen, if you look to the right of the aircraft you can see us coming alongside Diamond Head, one of the two volcanoes that formed Oahu - home of Honolulu, Waikiki and Pearl Harbor. We will be landing shortly. Aloha and welcome to Hawaii."

Walking off the plane, I could smell the humidity and fresh scents of the indigenous flowers used to make leis. The airport was open-air, with large holes in the walls where windows usually would be. Everything seemed so basic and not at all what I had been expecting, but the tropical views of the ocean and palm trees everywhere were absolutely breathtaking.

My shuttle arrived at Pearl Harbor Naval Base late in the afternoon and I checked into the Bachelor Officers' Quarters, or BOQ, which are similar to a hotel without the service or amenities. It would be my temporary home for a few weeks until I settled on a place to live. The room was small and somewhat dingy, not unlike something seen from movies made in the 1960s such as *Blue Hawaii* with Elvis or *The Last Stand* with John Wayne. I cracked open the windows and let the luscious air flow in. There was no air conditioner in the room, which was common in Hawaii but something I had to get used to. I was taking the new environment all in, and I was so giddy, I couldn't stand staying inside. I wanted to get out and explore this brand-new world.

My boat, the USS *Birmingham*, was still at sea and was expected to arrive in port within a few days. Since I had time to spare, I did all my check-ins on the base and around town, such as registering myself with the medical office and getting the appropriate pass for my car. Squadron Seven, which was the office that managed the USS *Birmingham* as well as eight other submarines stationed in Hawaii, informed me of the precise date and time for *Birmingham's* arrival. According to instructions, I was to be standing on the pier side in my khaki uniform upon its arrival and report to the captain once docked.

I was getting hungry after my day of errands, so I decided to grab lunch at the Yacht Club on base, which was recommended by one of the Squadron staff members. The drive was short and through an industrial part of the base to the back side of Pearl Harbor. It was a beautiful day, so I asked the host to seat me outside on the deck that overlooked the harbor. The wooden deck was on the second floor and covered by a white canopy that provided shade from the noon sun. I sat on a wicker chair in the corner at a small table. To my right, I could see just above the shrubs and small trees below to the wide open harbor. On the horizon, the far corner of the island was reaching into the deep blue Pacific Ocean, and between it and me was Ford Island, resting in the middle of Pearl Harbor. Ford Island is best known as the historic site where the USS *Arizona* was tied pier-side during the Japanese attack on Pearl Harbor on December 4, 1941. From my view, I could see the white, rectangular-shaped Arizona Memorial sitting just above the water. The history of this island and the service I was embarking on for my country had a profound effect on me as I absorbed the sights in my view.

***

The day of my reporting to the submarine, I woke up around 5 a.m. to get ready, went through my shave and shower routine, and dressed in my khaki uniform. I headed from the BOQ to the nearest mess hall on base, a two-block walk from where I stayed. The morning was shaking out to be a typical beautiful day in Hawaii. The sun was already midway up the horizon and the sky was all blue with no clouds in sight. I entered the mess hall and loaded my plate with a hearty breakfast so I would not get hungry later. Following breakfast, I walked around the base to kill time until the boat arrived. Eventually, I meandered to the submarine piers where I was to wait for the arrival of USS *Birmingham*.

I could see the submarine start to approach the pier from afar. It looked amazing, just as I had envisioned: a sleek, dark-hulled boat with 90 percent of its mass below the water. The only prominent aspect of the boat on the surface was the sail, a boxy-shaped unit about halfway down the centerline of the boat. A razor-shaped rudder on the aft end cut the water as the whitewashed ocean left a longer trail than the length of the boat. "Single up all lines!" a chief standing topside yelled.

There were a few other crew members standing along the pier with me, so I used the opportunity to learn what I was supposed to do when I crossed the bow. Petty Officer Marco Valdez was the first person I met pier-side and he informed me that I was to cross the bow and salute the ensign, which is the U.S. flag tied to the aft of the boat, and then salute the captain before I went aboard. I made my salutes, sharp and swift, and then said in as sturdy a voice as I could muster, "Lieutenant Elguindi reporting as ordered, sir!" The Captain, Commander J.B. Cassias at the time, gave me a look over then said, "Very well. Get below and check in with the Engineer." My heart was pounding so hard I could feel my chest start to ache. All these people dressed in blue and khaki were crawling out of the two holes of the submarine like ants climbing out of an anthill that had just been disturbed.

I climbed down the ladder and asked my way around to find the Engineer's quarters. The hallway was a passageway so narrow that two men could not pass by each other without stepping sideways. I walked

61

about thirty feet down the passageway and took a sharp left to find the wardroom. The wardroom was the main area where the officers got together. During meals it was set up as a dining area and by day it was used for everything from training to a hospital table in case of emergencies. I glanced in, looking for my way, and someone pointed me around the corner to the last stateroom. These "staterooms" were about the size of a walk-in closet, yet they housed three officers, usually some of the senior guys stationed on the boat. My sense of stately luxury was about to take a sharp adjustment.

As I turned, I saw a man literally getting pushed, almost hurled, from the very stateroom I was pointed toward. A talk, dark-haired man with squinty eyes who I would later learn was my chief engineer, Lieutenant Commander Lee Hankins, was yelling at someone for something that I could barely understand, barring his final statement, "Get the hell out of here and fix the goddamn thing before you report back to me!" Then he took his gold-rimmed glasses off and said to me, "You Elguindi?" "Yes, sir," I uttered, nearly peeing in my pants. "Get the hell in here, now!" My first day aboard the USS *Birmingham* had begun.

Chapter 10
- My First Deployment -

Once I completed my boat check-in, Lieutenant Commander Hankins showed me around. I came to learn that the gruff exterior was not who he really was but a façade he created to get the tough job of chief engineer on a nuclear submarine done without flaw. He expected nothing short of perfection and the measuring stick for himself could not have been set higher by another person. He introduced me to the other officers stationed on the boat and I was inducted appropriately during our first meal. As part of submarine tradition, before they leave sub school, each officer is to write a letter to the boat welcoming its arrival. Little did I know that letter was sent around to each officer to make humorous comments regarding its content and grammar. The letter was passed around during lunch and everyone got their laughs. It was a fun bonding moment and I instantly knew this would be my family for the next three years of duty.

When a new junior officer joins the boat he is assigned to a slightly more senior junior officer whom they officially call a "sea-dad." The sea-dad is there to orient the newcomer and introduce him to other members of the boat. My sea-dad was Lieutenant Tony Sugalski. Tony was a tall, thin guy who was a couple years older than me. Tony became a good friend and helped me with my qualifications and advancement on the boat.

That weekend Tony and some other young officers took me out on the town. Walking along Kalakaua Avenue parallel to Waikiki

Beach was a sensation and sight I will never forget. It truly felt like Paradise Island, a dream considering where I had come from and how much I had overcome to get where I was. The April night was crystal clear and I could see so many stars and the crescent moon reflecting off the dark Pacific Ocean at night. We went to the popular local restaurant, Duke's, for dinner. It was named after a famous Hawaiian known as the "Father of modern surfing." Later that evening we strolled to Rainbow Row, a popular hotspot for nightlife, and hit a few dance clubs until the early hours of the morning.

After arriving in Hawaii, I had only a little more than a week to find a place to live and settle in before my boat went out to sea for my first deployment. Steve, a junior officer transferred to Hawaii at the same time as I was, and I decided to find a house to share together. In the few days before my departure, we rented a small three-bedroom house in Makakilo, a local town north of Barber's Point on the southern coast of Oahu, about eighteen miles from Pearl Harbor. Steve was a small, dark-haired man from New Jersey. He studied electrical engineering and liked to keep to himself most of the time. He chose Makakilo for its quaint community and isolation from the navy base. Given that we were not going to spend much time at home anyway, I didn't mind.

Makakilo was a series of small subdivisions that crawled up the mountainous arms of Hawaii, the top reaching into the blue sky. Coming down the mountain one day, I passed a church at the bottom of the hill, Makakilo Baptist Church, and made a point to check it out before I left for sea.

On Monday morning, I learned that the exercise we would be doing involved an international joint exercise with the Japanese, Canadian, Korean and Australian navies for what was known as RIMPAC 94. This naval training exercise was similar to a game of Risk, where everyone brought their elements of warfare together, then split up into two teams, Blue and Gold. The combined teams set sail for forty-five days to conduct a mock sea-going war so that each unit could refine their wartime tactics and practice operations with other naval vessels.

64

During that operation, I worked extremely hard to get all my qualifications for Engineering Officer of the Watch (EOOW). Every junior officer had to complete his qualifications as soon as possible so that he could stand watch. Watch rotations happened every six hours and the EOOW was responsible for managing the nuclear reactor and supporting personnel during steaming operations. The addition of a watch officer to the ship's rotation helped ease the responsibility of standing watch for the officers. I completed my qualifications in one of the shortest time periods for a junior officer and was eager to start standing watch and contributing to the boat.

At sea our days were long. Officers' muster was usually around 0600 hours, military time for 6:00 a.m. The day started with breakfast and preparation in the wardroom. After breakfast we began training drills where we practiced various scenarios that might occur in an emergency at sea. Sea-time Readiness, or the proficiency to handle these drills, was a critical part of our regular training. Training drills included such things as encountering an enemy submarine, on-board fire while under way, and nuclear accidents. Drills lasted about three hours and were followed by a training debrief in the wardroom. During the week we usually did two drill sets a day, one in the morning and one in the afternoon. At 1730 hours, we mustered in the wardroom for supper and then I quickly departed as junior wardroom officer to go relieve the current EOOW and take my watch from 1800 to 2400 hours. When my watch ended around midnight, I was relieved by the next oncoming EOOW. Following my watch, I went to the wardroom again since they served midrats, the Navy version of a late-night snack, about that time.

The boat was generally quiet late at night, so I used the opportunity to catch up on my administrative duties and advanced qualifications. Every officer onboard had additional responsibility of managing a division. A division usually consisted of four to twenty personnel who managed a particular aspect of the boat. My first division was a small one called IC division, which managed all the interior communications such as phone and speaker circuits. I later advanced to RC division, which oversaw all electronic aspects of the nuclear reactor, and then Assistant Navigator and Operations, where I became intimately familiar with planning and charting our operations in the Pacific Ocean. My advanced qualifications involved becoming Officer of the Deck (OOD) qualified. The OOD was the most significant watch station for an officer on the boat. As OOD we were directly responsible for effectively "driving" the boat, which meant following charted courses and providing guidance and direction to personnel to actually maneuver the submarine at sea.

Just a few months after reporting to the *Birmingham*, we received a new Commanding Officer to lead our boat. Commander Mark W. Kenny relieved the CO of two years, Commander Jeffery Casias, in November of that year. Mark recalls the following:

> *The crew of* Birmingham *had a great reputation when I arrived in October 1994. Led by their skipper, now Rear Admiral Jeff Cassias and their Chief of the Boat, now Master Chief Steve "Soup" Campbell, they were a formal, well-trained, and disciplined crew. I interviewed all the officers prior to my taking command of the ship on 6 November 1994. Nader at the time was onboard for six to eight months and was standing watches on the reactor plant while working on his qualifications in submarines. He impressed me first by his military appearance and demeanor. Close-cropped hair, crisp uniform, athletic appearance and gung-ho personality. I remember that he told me he planned to be the first U.S. Navy admiral of Arab-Persian-American descent. That struck me as a little bit cocky, but I liked his attitude and vision. I was glad he was going to be a valuable member of the officer leadership on the ship when I assumed command.*

Later that same month in November, we docked at Pearl Harbor Naval Shipyard for a four-month maintenance procedure known as SRA. An SRA meant that our submarine went into dry dock, effectively hauling it out of the water so that we could conduct a scheduled resin discharge maintenance procedure, which occurred for all nuclear submarines in our class once every ten years. Since this was an infrequent evolution, we had to take extreme caution in managing this procedure. The engineering officers were stationed on port and starboard watches, which meant we were to watch over the maintenance and nuclear reactor every other twelve-hour segment.

The maintenance evolution was going smoothly and I recall our last day on port and starboard watches. Lieutenant Ed Meintzer and I were stationed on the afternoon watch Saturday, November 19, 1994. We had completed the last operation for resin discharge ahead of schedule and had proceeded to contact the Chief Engineer and Captain, requesting to stand down from the rigorous watch. We were given the appropriate authorization, and Ed and I both decided to finish work we had left, shifting to standard Ship Duty Officer rotation whereby normal twenty-four-hour watches at port would resume. I was relieved of my duties around four in the morning on Sunday and decided to head home for some rest in my own house rather than sleep on the boat.

I recall revving up my motorcycle in the gravel lot next to the shipyard. It was a cool night, and I headed off base back to my house in Makakilo. The trek was eighteen miles and usually went quickly since most of it was freeway. But, unfortunately, that was my last clear memory. Everything else is a blur.

CHAPTER 11
- LIEUTENANT EDWARD MEINTZER -

Nader Elguindi asked me to briefly recount the day of his accident, told from my perspective and how I best remembered it. The event took place quite a few years ago, and my memory is not what I would hope it to be, but I believe nonetheless that I've accurately portrayed the events of the day in this selection. Most important to me is that Nader has triumphed over his adversity. If this piece assists Nader with his efforts in inspiring others to do the same, then it is with great pleasure that I share this with you.

I remember the day of Nader's accident as a particularly difficult one. First of all, Nader and I had duty on the weekend. Weekends are generally slower days on a submarine that is in port due to the fact that only about one-fourth of the crew is onboard, and therefore the activity is typically less. Sailors that have weekend duty can generally expect to have a somewhat less harried day than might otherwise be the case during the weekdays. Unfortunately, however, our submarine was going through some complicated repair and maintenance evolutions to get ready to go out to sea. Because Nader and I were the only two officers on duty or even on the ship that day, we were particularly busy because we were responsible for managing everything that took place onboard.

A minor annoyance for me, but an irritant that put me in a foul mood for duty that day, was the fact that the duty schedule had been set up in a way that was particularly unfavorable to me. There are two roles for officers on duty on a submarine in port. The first role is called the "Ships Duty Officer," or the officer responsible for the whole ship, and generally the senior officer was scheduled for this role. The other role is the "Engineering Duty Officer," who was focused on activities related to the engine room. This role reported to the Ships Duty Officer, and because of this, was typically the junior officer on duty. I was senior to Nader in terms of rank and experience on the ship. In fact, I believe that Nader had just recently qualified as Ships Duty Officer. That being the case, I was piqued when I was scheduled as the Engineering Duty Officer and Nader as Ships Duty Officer for the day. These details might appear trivial to the uninitiated; however, both Nader and I knew better. If all or even most of the maintenance planned got completed, the Engineering Duty Officer could "double up" the duty and act as both the Ships Duty Officer and the Engineering Duty Officer. In other words, the Ships Duty Officer could be sent home to enjoy his weekend. Therefore, Nader had a reasonable possibility, depending on our ability to move forward with the tasks that were scheduled, of going home that day, whereas I knew I would be spending my night on the boat.

With that as background, I remember little of the details of the day, other than the fact that I spent the majority of my time in the engine room digging into the details of a number of particularly grueling maintenance projects. I think I got out of the engine room a couple of times to eat lunch and dinner, and to simultaneously visit with Nader as he ate his meals. We talked with one another intermittently via the ship's communication system about the various activities we were engaged in. Mainly I remember giving Nader status reports on our progress, so that he would be updated and able to inform our captain about milestones reached, and also requesting permission from him as the acting Ships Duty Officer to conduct certain procedures. I quite clearly recall feeling sorry about not being able to send Nader home at a reasonable hour, but I was busy enough in the engine room that I didn't feel comfortable "doubling up" Nader until later. The activity didn't really seem to subside until around midnight. Because we were both exhausted at the time, I remember thinking that it would be the safe and responsible thing to do to ask him to stay through until the end of the duty day the next morning. However, I knew that Nader was looking forward to going home, and I would have wanted to leave myself if I had been in his position, so I agreed to take the Ships Duty Officer role from him. He spent a few hours finishing up a maintenance routine and left for home around 4 a.m.

I've often looked back on my decision to relieve Nader of his duty. It seems cruel to me that an act of kindness, even an act as small and perfunctory as it was, could lead to what occurred. I know now that Nader should not have been on the road that night, and fully regret my lack of judgment in giving him the option to leave earlier.

Soon after Nader was gone, some shipyard personnel approached me about some work they wanted to do on a critical valve that needed some rework. I remember spending some time with them around the valve, and finally going to bed around 3:00 a.m. I recall thinking that I would have to get up at 5:30 a.m. to do my 6:00 a.m. tour, and fully expected to spend the whole next day sleeping to recover from such a brutal duty night.

At 5:30 a.m., I was up and about, albeit moving slowly. I had decided not to shave that morning just so I could have some extra time to sleep. I think I failed to shave on duty days maybe twice during my naval career as I personally viewed it as a sign of a lack of professionalism. I mention this only as an indication of how tired I was. Basically, another few minutes of sleep were more important to me than grooming. In other words, I fully understand how Nader fell asleep on his bike that night; I likely would have done the same.

Because nothing much had changed since midnight, my tour of the engine room that morning (around 6:00 a.m.) went like clockwork. I started forward to begin my tour of the front of the ship, so that I could complete my duty day and turnover to the incoming duty section. As I was walking forward, I came upon Tony Sugalski, the officer who was to relieve me as the incoming Ships Duty Officer. As usual, Tony had made it to the ship early so that he could come to a full understanding of the status of the ship before assuming the watch.

He had been in the wardroom, and indicated that he had taken a call from a nearby military hospital. He informed me that Nader had crashed his motorcycle and was in critical condition at the hospital. Very few other details were available.

I was sick with guilt, and with fear of the possibilities. I finished my tour in an almost catatonic state, turned over to Tony, and called the captain to inform him of Nader's accident. The Captain was of course concerned about Nader, and asked several questions about his condition. Because the hospital had provided very little information to me or Tony, I was unable to answer many of them. This only made me feel even more guilty and powerless. There was little I could do but pray that Nader would be alright.

Later, after several surgeries and while Nader's life still hung in the balance, I went to visit him at the hospital. Nader was not conscious in any true sense of the word, and the bottom half of his body was mangled. In the end, with the support of Nader's family, it was decided to amputate his leg to save his life.

I will bear witness to the fact that Nader has overcome his injury. He is personable, successful, and clearly enjoys life to the fullest. That being said, Nader's the best person to tell the rest of his story, as his journey truly began where I've left off.

Stage Three:
Climbing the Mountains

CHAPTER 12
- THE CHRISTMAS PARTY -

Back at the hospital, I was downgraded to the orthopedic ward after spending almost two weeks in intensive care. The move to the seventh floor was a huge lift for me - intensive care had been a morbid environment, and it was a relief to be out of there. Although my dad had gone back to his work and family in Massachusetts and my mom had returned to her work in Georgia, by the third week following my accident, my sister had moved out to Hawaii. Nellie had been attending the University of North Carolina at Charlotte, studying for her Master's degree in environmental science. She decided to finish her semester early and move to Hawaii to help care for and support me. She moved into my old room at my house in Makakilo but spent most of her time during the day at Tripler Hospital. Her presence was very uplifting, but the gravity of the situation was still difficult to handle.

The balloons and flowers that everyone had sent were starting to wither away and I felt the weight of time passing with little physical progress. I was on my back twenty-four hours a day and still had not gained much mobility. My left leg was in a metal contraption that kept it lifted off the bed, and the staples keeping my abdomen together from my first day of emergency operations looked like railroad tracks from my waist to my heart.

One of the well-known side effects of amputations is a syndrome called phantom pains. To put it simply, phantom pain is the name for the phenomenon of feeling pain in the limb that was lost. Many doctors used to believe that phantom pain was a figment of the patient's imagination brought on by the extreme psychological stress of losing the limb. However, it has been found that phantom pain is a real reaction to the trauma that has been inflicted on the nerves. Part of the amputation process is to cut the nerve endings high above the end of the amputated limb by "plucking" them so they do not hit the surface area when a patient starts wearing a prosthetic. Nerve cells do not regenerate like other parts of our body, such as skin that grows back together when it has been cut, so the nerve endings go through a process to reorient themselves to their new condition and environment. Phantom sensations can range from mild tingling to severe stabbing pains that have driven people to want to die rather than live with the pain. I started to develop these odd pains a few days after the surgery in which they amputated my foot. I would wake up in the middle of the night, intensely wanting to scratch an itch on a foot that was no longer there.

With all the time spent lying in a hospital bed, I started thinking about how complicated everything had become. Using the bathroom required the use of a plastic bottle by the bed; it was awkward and sometimes created a mess. Bowel movements were an embarrassing episode requiring assistance from the nurse and the use of a bedpan. The fact that I needed help for every minor function that was part of my independence was demoralizing. I felt like a shell of a person, far from normal and anything but capable. That was the first time I started to question God, asking, "Why me?" I didn't understand what was happening around me and could only dream about everything being normal again. Sleep was spotty and infrequent and some nights I would break down and weep for hours.

Fortunately, my friends wanted to help me stay positive and brought me inspirational stories of military personnel who survived traumatic injuries and came back to complete their duty. I still have the article of Carl M. Brashear, who was not only the first African American to become a U.S. Navy Master Diver, but also the first person to achieve that role with a prosthetic leg. In 1966, during recovery operations for a hydrogen bomb lost off the coast of Spain, a line used for towing broke loose, causing a pipe to strike Brashear's left leg below the knee with incredible force. He was evacuated to a series of hospitals, finally ending up at the Naval Hospital in Portsmouth, Virginia. Unrelenting infections and the promise of years of recovery led Brashear to convince his doctors to amputate the lower portion of his leg. In April 1968, Brashear became the first amputee to be certified as a diver, and in 1970 he became the first African American U.S. Navy Master Diver. He served for ten more years, eventually achieving the rank of Master Chief Boatswain's Mate. In 2000, Brashear's military service was portrayed by Cuba Gooding, Jr. in the film *Men of Honor.*

Master Chief Brashear's story and the family environment that the Navy provided motivated me to continue fighting. Getting my career back became the focus of my efforts. I had found a sense of home inside the cold, stark atmosphere of the submarine USS *Birmingham,* and the thought that if I could finish my qualifications in submarines, I could be whole again grew within me and encouraged me to persevere.

I made my desires official when the Navy liaison officer visited my room a couple of weeks after I arrived in the orthopedic ward. Her answer was sympathetic but direct. "We're waiting to see how your situation develops, but we need to start talking about the medical retirement process," she said. "You will be formally discharged and the VA will manage your health care for the rest of your life."

"But what will I do?" I asked. "What else *can* I do? The Navy is my life. This is who I am and what I want to be."

"Well, you can appeal our decision." She explained the process and then I was required to sign a release waiving my medical retirement. Instead of accepting the medical retirement, I opted to challenge the Physical Evaluation Board (PEB) to continue on active duty once I was healthy.

My Commanding Officer, Commander Mark W. Kenny, supported me unconditionally. He said, "Whatever it takes, Nader, we will be there for you." I cannot stress enough how instrumental Mark was in allowing me to continue my Navy career. In most cases, I would have been placed on TDRL, or Temporary Disability Retirement List, in a process to be discharged from the military. The USS *Birmingham*, as with any boat in the fleet, was assigned a certain number of officer billets, or positions they were allowed to fill in order to support their mission. If I was placed on TDRL, Mark would have freed up a billet and could have gotten a replacement for me to support the ship's staff. Instead, Mark allowed me to be placed on leave and assignment to our Squadron, which allowed me the time to recover without being immediately discharged. I learned long after my recovery that Mark and the USS *Birmingham* staff had to operate the submarine shorthanded to accommodate my desire to stay in the Navy.

With my mind set on trying to stay in the Navy, I needed to focus on improving physically and mentally. My energy gradually became renewed and I developed a sense of mission. The first objective I set was becoming mobile again. After some time, practice and help from my sister, I was able to move around with the assistance of a wheelchair. With some help, I could get from the bed to the chair where friends and family could wheel me around the hospital floors. This was my first opportunity to go outside the hospital room without being on a gurney. Nellie and I started exploring the halls of the hospital and occasionally went to the cafeteria to get our meals. My body was still frail, so I needed blankets to keep me warm and would be exhausted after sitting upright for an hour or more. Escaping the environment of the ward, even for a short period, was a huge step for me.

***

One day I got a visit from a woman, Cindy Bautista, who was not dressed as a doctor or nurse but looked like she was part of the hospital staff. Cindy was a captain in the Army and the head of physical therapy for Tripler Hospital. She informed me that I needed to start my physical therapy and scheduled me for an appointment the next morning.

The physical therapy room was on the ground floor of the hospital. It was a large area set up much like a gym except the equipment was oriented for recovering patients instead of athletes. There were exercise cycles and some small free weights, but the room was mostly full of mats and canvases. Going to physical therapy gave me something to look forward to on my path to getting healthy again.

When I arrived for my appointment, Cindy was there to greet me. She was a stout, young tomboy of a woman and very passionate about what she did. Frankly, she was tough as nails when it came to physical exercise and helping me drive toward my goal of mobility. Things started with simple flexibility exercises. I would begin with my upper body muscles or at least what was left of them. I tried moving my arms, reaching above my head in basic stretches just to extend those muscles. I sat on a large, matted table with several inches of cushion that kept my sensitive body parts from experiencing too much pain. With my amputated leg, Cindy would test the range of motion in my knee by bending the joint back as far as it could go. She told me that range of motion would be a very important factor in getting a good fit in a prosthetic when the time came.

Unfortunately, after the weeks on my back with little motion, my joints and tendons had stiffened and my muscles had atrophied. Cindy told me that this was a common problem. "Your body can build that movement and muscle back, but it takes time." We eventually moved from the platforms to the mats and after a while I was using small weights to rebuild muscle mass in my upper body. My progress became evident and I started to feel a little bit stronger. I was getting excited about the morning routines - each small improvement was a victory.

I was doing well enough after my first month in physical therapy that they wanted me to take a few steps on a test prosthetic. The thought made me nervous and excited at the same time. It was hard to imagine what the first time standing, being vertical and taking my first steps, would be like. I was looking forward to the day but it would not come quickly. First, they had to build a prosthetic that fitted my leg using a cast mold of my amputated stump. After the mold, they had to align the system with my height, weight and approximate gait. It took almost ten days to finish the bulky contraption.

I was wheeled into the physical therapy room and placed in front of the parallel bars to stabilize me while I walked. My left leg was still in traction so I was unable to bear any weight on it. The first few steps were actually going to be hops on this metal leg while balancing with my upper body by holding on to the bars. I was hoisted to a vertical position by Cindy and another physical therapist, who held me up by my arms then lowered me onto the new prosthetic. At first, my adrenaline was rushing so hard it was hard to stop myself from hopping as fast as possible. I took a deep breath to calm my nerves and slowly used my arms to move down the path between the parallel bars while putting as much weight as I could bear on the new leg. Just before reaching the end, I started to fall before the therapists caught me. My left leg jammed against the floor and I felt a jolt of pain resonate throughout my entire body. The right leg began bleeding again at the sutures that were holding the recently cut skin and muscle together. The two therapists helped me back into the chair, saying encouraging words, but my spirit was crushed. I had so much confidence going into the day, hoping to start using a prosthetic, but the pain and uphill battle were too overwhelming. I started to mope, wondering if the doctors and psychiatrists were right after all. Maybe I was dreaming.

The setback required me to wait until my left leg was able to share the weight. Maybe then I could start using the prosthetic.

I am sure it was apparent my hopes were fading. With the help of my sister and crew, we decided to focus on getting a day away from the hospital. I needed another goal, something within reach that would give me something to work toward. I had not left the campus of the hospital since I had arrived and my progress using a chair was improving. I was using fewer painkillers and was downgraded from the morphine IV drip to an oral narcotic called Tylox. It was not as strong as morphine and had fewer side effects. By this time we were well into December and my Captain invited me to join the crew of the USS *Birmingham* for our Christmas party. It was two weeks away and something we all felt was attainable.

We received permission from the doctors and staff to get one day's leave from the ward so I could attend the Christmas party. I took a couple of extra Tylox to help me with all the motion required for the transport to the party and got dressed into the most normal clothes I could muster. This was not an easy task since at the hospital it was easy to let myself go. I went days, sometimes weeks, without shaving and often wore the same t-shirt and boxer shorts under my hospital blanket each day. But this day, I cleaned myself up as well as I could and put on a real shirt and shorts. After all, it was still Hawaii. My sister helped me into the car, a forest green Jeep Cherokee. She drove the two miles from the hospital to the yacht club where the boat party was being held. We pulled into the parking lot of the restaurant after the party had already started because it had taken us a while to get everything going. Nellie rolled the wheelchair to the passenger side of the Cherokee and I used the arm handle and car seat to leverage my way from the car into the chair. With everything in place, we took the elevator up one flight of stairs into the restaurant the Captain had rented out for the party. All the crew was socializing, having drinks and fun. Commander Kenny and his wife, Cheryl, were the first to greet me, welcoming my surprise visit to the party.

I was so enthusiastic to be back around my friends, regardless of the circumstances. That day was my own - I was a normal person for a couple of hours. Many crew members who were not able to visit me at the hospital used the time to catch up. I felt at home, like it was family. My motivation was reinvigorated and I wanted to be back.

After a short stay at the party, we had to start making the trip back to the hospital. I said goodbye to all my friends and told them to keep a seat warm for me. My sister loaded me back into the Cherokee, but just before we started to roll off, one of the crew members, Petty Officer Wagner, came to the passenger side window to talk. Wagner was an "A-ganger," as we referred to them on the boat. They were auxiliary mechanics, some of the biggest and burliest guys on the boat. They were the men who operated the large diesel engines that the boat used as backup power in case of emergencies. "I'm sorry. I wasn't there for you, and I apologize," he said.

I was in shock, not sure what he meant. "Don't be silly. It's not your fault," I said. Wagner went on: "Do you remember when you were just getting started on the boat? You came down to the machinery room. You were doing a tour and we were working on the diesel. There was a deck plate open and you weren't paying attention. I caught you just before you fell into the well. I was looking out for you. I always look out for my crew and I was not there for you that night." As he was hanging on to the window sill, Wagner's eyes began watering.

I was completely taken aback by my friend's emotion. He had only known me a few months, yet he had a great sense of duty and obligation because I was a member of his crew. We exchanged a few more stories and I assured him I would be back. "You can be there for me next time," I said. "I'll need you, so make sure you stick around because I am coming back!"

After the Christmas party, I went back to my routine at the hospital. With each improvement, I became more optimistic about my chances. December was capped off by spending New Year's Eve in a room on the sea side of Tripler Hospital. Tripler sat on the Kona (southern) side of a mountain north of the harbor. From a seaside room we could see the deep blue Pacific Ocean just across the plains of the island, and Honolulu was visible in the distance to the west. New Year's Eve was a special celebration in Hawaii, and one of the most fantastic fireworks shows I have ever seen was on this night. My sister and I turned the lights out and enjoyed a quiet evening in awe. I could see the light at the end of the tunnel and was eager to move on.

As January progressed, I was learning to do things on my own. I could climb in and out of the wheelchair on my own. There was a handicapped-accessible bathroom that I began using without assistance from the nurses. My spirits were high but I still required regular use of Tylox. One of the staff physicians was becoming concerned with my use of the narcotic and raised the issue with me. "I want to start weaning you off the drug," he said. I nodded and agreed to take less medication. By the next morning, the nurses came in to administer my meds and Tylox was no longer on the prescription. It had been completely eliminated from my prescriptions. I asked what happened and the nurse informed me that the doctor decided to stop cold turkey.

I was addicted.

The next thirty-six hours were painful as I went through withdrawal without the aid of anything to bring me down. By the afternoon, my body was breaking into cold sweats. The pain from the withdrawal was so great that it masked any physical pain I was experiencing. Around midnight the shakes began, and they kept me awake until dawn. The next morning, I was finally able to hold down some water. By noon the shakes had stopped and my withdrawal was finally over. It was clear to me how much the narcotics had taken hold of my body. I was helpless and had unknowingly relinquished control of my body to the drug. I wanted to be in control of my body at all times, and it was the best way to ensure my speediest recovery.

Near the end of January, I was released from the hospital. The doctors felt that living with my sister's care back at my own house would be good for me. The environment around the ward was depressing and not helping me focus on getting better. I was excited to get back to my own house, where I had privacy and comforts that I had not seen in three months.

We had to make several modifications to allow me to stay at home, and my dad returned to Hawaii to help my sister and roommate get the house ready for me. There was a two-inch ledge at the

83

back door, so my dad and roommate built a small ramp that allowed me to go in and out of the house in a wheelchair. Our hallways were too narrow for the chair, so we had to find a bed for the living room. Since my own bed was a waterbed, it wasn't practical to move it, but my neighbors donated an old spare bed for me to use, which we placed in the corner of the living room. In our house, the living and dining area made up one large area, and my bed fit into the corner without taking up too much space, so things worked out well.

I spent the majority of my days at home, resting on my bed and the couch. It is amazing how much TV I was able to catch up on. Since the weather in Hawaii is generally sunny and warm, I was also able to go outside frequently. A short venture into the yard to soak up a little sun was tremendously rewarding. The fact my accident occurred in Hawaii played a large role in my positive recovery.

Nellie and I managed to get by fairly well. We would get ready in the morning and she would drive me to the hospital. I would spend the better part of the day at physical therapy working out and trying to keep my body limber and strong. I made doctor visits as necessary and was lined up with an occupational therapist to care for my non-functioning left arm. The nerve damage was not permanent but would require several years to adjust.

At home, Nellie would prepare meals that I was able to handle. She and I would make the trek to the grocery store to pick up things for dinner and sometimes a movie to help time pass. Steve, my roommate, was at sea most of the time, so we had the house to ourselves. One evening we were running late and both of us were hungry, so we stopped by the grocery store to pick up a roasted chicken and some bread for dinner. As we turned the corner around one of the aisles, a native Hawaiian woman and her friend stopped in front of me. "Are you Nader?" she asked.

I was startled that she knew my name. "Yes," I said. She replied, "I'm the one who found you that night." I sat motionless for a moment, completely shocked. I had read the police report dozens of times, trying to put together what had happened, but the details were sketchy and there was only a vague reference to "a couple finding me and calling 911." No one had been able to determine the cause or circumstance of the accident, and there were no firsthand accounts other than those of this mystery couple.

And here she was - standing in front of me three months later.

She was so nice and concerned for me, saying that she could not believe I was alive. "You were conscious when we found you, but the paramedics thought you had little chance of making it. You had lost so much blood." She expressed her happiness that I was alive and we talked for what must have been half an hour. I got her number and she agreed to talk with me some more. I had so many questions. I wanted to know what had happened.

She was able to fill me in on as much detail as I know today. At 5 a.m. on Sunday, November 20, 1994, they were returning from a local party and noticed a motorcycle idling by the side of the road. Seeing no one around, she climbed a mound where she discovered me lying there, both of my legs severed below the knee. My motorcycle had collided with the exit sign for Makakilo Drive, my turn to go home and only one mile from my neighborhood. As my motorcycle idled on the highway, the front light burning, I lay on the grass for what was estimated to be twenty to twenty-five minutes. I am so fortunate that this young couple saw the motorcycle and stopped. Their care is one of the miracles that I thank God for every day.

After talking with this woman, I knew that I would never find out what had caused my accident, but I finally felt at ease with what had happened. There was nothing I could do to change the past, but my future was in front of me and I felt more ready than ever to start living again.

A few weeks after I was staying back at my own home, Brian Wallace, my best friend from college, came to visit us in Hawaii for a week. He and Nellie would regularly talk on the phone and he wanted to help cheer me up. Although things were improving I was still in a tough place mentally. The wheelchair provided some freedoms, but the future of my physical capabilities was frail. While Brian was visiting we tried to go visit some popular places and locations, since Hawaii was so new to him. It gave us a chance to get out and explore, which I had not done since first arriving on the island.

One day we all packed some gear and went to Waikiki Beach. It was a nice day in Oahu with cool Kona breezes coming from the ocean, keeping the temperature in the low 80s. There was a concrete dock at the end of the beach and I decided to wheel myself that way while Nellie and Brian walked on the sand to get the long-needed stress relief she deserved. As I rolled down the dock, I recalled a day not long ago when I had gone scuba diving off the same beach. I loved the ocean and soaked up every opportunity to get in the water. Being near the ocean provided some relief, but when I saw kids playing in the water surfing and swimming, I became depressed. It was going to be months, maybe years, before I could get in the ocean again. I wanted to go swimming so badly and seeing everyone around me having a good time made things worse.

A young, dark-skinned Hawaiian kid, maybe twelve or thirteen, was sitting at the end of the dock. His eyes were locked on me in the wheelchair. What remained of my legs were exposed and it was evident how bad things were. He came up to me and stood in front of my chair for about a minute before speaking. "What happened, bruddah?" he asked. Hawaiian people have an interesting version of English that they use as slang. *Bruddah* and *sistah* are common greetings to any person. I sat silent for some time. I was feeling miserable enough and didn't welcome such open talking with a stranger. I'm sure a certain part of me wanted to shed my misery on the world. Finally, his patience wore mine out. "I was bitten by a shark in these very waters," I lied, pointing out over the ocean. The boy's eyes got very large and he scrambled to get up from the dock and run away. "You better not go surfing here. It could get you, too!" I yelled after him.

Unleashing my pain on a perfect stranger did nothing to help me. I felt worse for traumatizing a child who was only curious. I felt terrible and promised myself never to do that again. I had gone through something horrific, but it was my burden to bear. I vowed to share it with others in a positive light one day.

After this day, I tried even harder to seem cheerful - strangers saw me as upbeat. I could tell they often wanted to ask how I could be so happy. But I was only burying my misery deep inside myself, and it continued to build. On the outside, I didn't want to let anyone down. On the inside, the burden was becoming overwhelming. I used the confines of my private home to release my tension. I became grouchy and unbearable at times. My sister, being my full-time caretaker, took the brunt of my frustrations. She is a strong person but I know how I acted hurt her. Sometimes, when I became angry, it was like watching events unfold in a movie that I had no control over. I felt detached and helpless. And after blowing up, I just beat myself up more for taking it out on the one person who had dedicated her days to helping me.

Things finally came to a head one day when we were grocery shopping. Nellie was wheeling me down one of the aisles of the grocery store. We stopped to pick up some soy sauce for a dinner she was preparing. "Can you get the green one?" I asked. "Why?" she replied. "I like the red one." And the fight began.

I wanted green and she wanted red. We were getting louder and louder and people around us were starting to stare. Something so trivial, but it was the culmination of three months of tension. No one was meant to bear what she had been going through - giving up so much, being so far away from everything familiar to her. My frustrations were being taken out on her, and since she had a kind and passive personality, she rarely defended herself. So we ended up fighting over soy sauce. It was the end - she was ready to go home.

My physical capabilities were dramatically improving and I could even get in and out of the Jeep without assistance. We mutually decided that I should be on my own; it was the only way I would get better. I needed to deal with my misery without the aid of others.

That next week, Nellie packed her clothes and things. We loaded the Jeep and I drove her to Honolulu International Airport. The goodbye was short - she just grabbed her bags from the back seat and waved. I said, "Safe flight. Call me when you land." In that moment, I was deeply saddened by what was happening to me and what I was becoming.

CHAPTER 13
- LEARNING TO WALK AGAIN -

Managing things on my own, I learned to push the limits of my physical capabilities. I started making strides that advanced my mobility more and faster than I thought would have been possible. I was caring for myself in my home and preparing meals on my own, and in the mornings, I would even drive myself to the hospital so I could attend physical therapy.

Me getting in and out of my car had to be an unusual sight for anyone who happened to see it. I would wheel my chair to the back of the Cherokee and pop the hatch button that was located in the bottom middle of the back door. It was close to the bumper, so it was easy to reach. I would then crawl out of the chair and onto the ground without using my legs or having them touch the ground other than my heel, which I used for balance. I would fold the chair and, using my upper body, lift it into the back of the car. I had tied a small rope to the back of the hatch that I could reach while sitting on the ground so I could close the hatch from this odd sitting position. It would take a great effort, but with some practice I got good at pulling the door down and slamming it shut. I would then hobble on my arms to the driver's door, pulling myself forward with my elbows, and lift myself into the car. Fortunately, my left leg was braced and able to withstand a small amount of pressure. I used it for pressing the gas and brake pedals while my right stump, hardly a leg anymore, was shifted to the right of the chair and out of the way. Getting out was a similar exercise in reverse. It wasn't pretty, but it was functional. Despite the awkwardness, it was a great feeling to get around independently.

The surgery to reconstruct my left leg was scheduled for late February and the days were soon approaching. Dr. Ono designed a unique surgery called a tibia-calcanus fusion whereby he would mend my tibia, the large bone in the lower leg, with the heel of my foot by using a bone graft to fuse the two pieces together. During the accident, the ankle joint in my left foot had been displaced, so I was not able to move my foot at all. The proposed fusion would create a single bone that ran from my knee to my heel without a moving joint, but it would allow me to bear weight on that leg. That surgery went smoothly and I came out of it with no pins in my left leg and a new fiberglass cast.

Within one week of the surgery, the doctors had me holding on to parallel bars and slowly trying to put weight on the cast. Things started slowly with only a mild amount of pressure, but within a few days, I was able to stand on the cast supported by parallel bars for balance only. I gained a lot of confidence with my reconstructed foot and started walking back and forth between the bars on the cast. I felt like my body was being put back together in slow motion.

Soon I was able to bear my full weight and walk on the cast. The next day I went to physical therapy, and Cindy informed me that it was time to test the prosthesis again. My initial steps were small since I had not gained my confidence back from falling when I first tried walking on the prosthetic, but this time, things started to slowly improve and after a few days, I could get around with the use of crutches. Walking was awkward, but I managed. My armpits started to get sore from the rub of the wooden crutches, so one of my friends at physical therapy fitted me with lofstran crutches, which wrapped around my forearms instead and made it easier for me get around. At times I still needed the wheelchair to go long distances but I was finally able to stand and walk around a small room on my own.

In the months following my ability to walk with crutches, I spent spare time volunteering at Makakilo Baptist Church. I enjoyed working with the youth and struck up a friendship with Steve Phillips, the church's youth pastor. Steve had been a Navy pilot stationed at Barbers Point Naval Air Station in Hawaii just a few years earlier. Then, at age twenty-six, he had a seizure. It turned out that he had a rare form of epilepsy that had gone unnoticed during his youth and the physical exams the military requires. Because pilots had such demanding responsibilities in the Navy, he was not allowed to continue with such a serious medical condition and it resulted in his medical retirement from the military. Steve and his wife, Laurie, first moved back to Kansas, where they had grown up, but less than a year later they chose to come back to Makakilo, where Steve got a job as the youth pastor to the church.

Steve was an athletic, mild-mannered, brown-haired guy. He liked basketball, football and the outdoors, so we had a lot in common. He also served as a great mentor and sounding board for me while I was going through my personal trials, fighting back from my injury to rejoin my crew on the *Birmingham*. Steve was a patient and calm person who provided a balanced contrast to my more gregarious personality. The time we spent with the Makakilo youth helped distract me from the daily complications that were engulfing my personal life.

By May, my mobility on crutches had improved enough that I requested to go back to work. I checked in with the Squadron office that managed my submarine, since my boat was busy at sea. In addition, the *Birmingham* had assigned me as temporary duty to the Squadron while I was still recovering from the accident. The chief of staff assigned me to an administrative job, working with the yeoman. I was given a small desk in one of the back offices and immediately put myself to work. Most of my duties were able to be completed from my desk so I would not have to spend too much time standing. I was given access to a computer and used my spare time to learn my way around the new systems.

One day, Carl, a staff member in the office mentioned the name of a Marine on the island, Bill Johnston, who had also lost his leg in a motorcycle accident. He told me that Bill had continued his career as a Marine and was still working at CINCPAC headquarters in Hawaii. (CINCPAC is the head of all Navy, Marine, Army and Air Force military operations in the Pacific.) I asked Carl for the number and kept it by my desk for several days, nervous about calling.

During the morning hours of most weekdays, I still visited physical therapy at Tripler Hospital. After spending a few hours working out what I could, I would head to the Squadron office to work for the day. While working there, I was an extra hand so my contributions were welcomed by the Squadron staff. At first, I was assigned simple administrative tasks to assist others. However, having tasks I could complete greatly improved my mental spirit. I felt like I was getting things done, and I wanted to keep moving up in my career. In my spare time, I studied for the submarine qualifications since access to all the confidential and secret material necessary was readily available at the Squadron.

Submarine qualifications are a series of actions, both simulated and academic, tests called "check-offs" that every submariner has to complete in order to earn his "dolphins." Dolphins are a submarine insignia centered above the left breast pocket and above the medals, worn at all times by officers and men qualified in submarine duty. The insignia itself is a bronze, gold-plated metal pin of the bow view of a submarine, proceeding on the surface, flanked by dolphins in a horizontal position with their heads resting on the upper edge of the bow planes. The dolphins insignia represents the small brotherhood of Submariners and is a symbol of the trust shipmates have in each individual to do the right thing to get the job done.

The check-offs themselves are like quizzes or short tests, and they cover the full range of electrical and mechanical systems onboard the submarines to procedures related to operating the boat both under way and at port. Each test require several days of preparation or study of the respective system or procedure. These check-offs literally have to be signed by a person who is a designated expert for that system, so I was quite lucky to be working at Squadron. Their staff consisted of approximately thirty senior enlisted men and officers - a large pool of people qualified to sign off on my various check-offs. The Submarine Qualification Book, or "qualbook," which contained the checklist of everything we were required to learn prior to our final exam, was a photocopied book of about thirty pages bound by two cardboard ends. Each page had the listing of five to ten check-offs that were to be completed for that section. Some steps involved preceding items being completed before moving forward, but many steps could be done in whichever order I desired. One of the Squadron staff, Lieutenant Commander Rick Low, helped me put a timeline and plan together to accomplish all my check-offs. Rick was the squadron engineer, which meant he was responsible for supporting all the engineers on the eight boats attached to the Squadron. His previous job was chief engineer on one of the submarines, so he was experienced in their issues and very bright himself, being selected for such a challenging position.

During downtime at the office, I would study the operations and procedures related to a particular check-off, then approach a submarine qualified officer on staff who would test me and sign me off once I completed it satisfactorily. I found out that many of the men on staff were more than helpful and I was truly encouraged being around them.

***

Unlike time on the boat, Squadron duty was a weekly day job. We would show up around 7:30 a.m. and wrap up our work by 1800 hours, or 6:00 p.m. Early on, my physical stamina was weak, and I found myself exhausted before the day was over. Afterwards, I would go home and just crash out for the evening. Often, I had to remind myself that I was still recovering from a major accident. My impatient mind wanted to go but my body was just not there yet.

As time passed, my strength and stamina improved and I was able to get around more efficiently, but many days were still difficult, especially mentally. During much of the first year after the accident,

I felt like an emotional yo-yo. I did not understand the process of recovering from an accident and amputation. Eventually I realized that I needed to talk with someone who had been through what I had. There were other amputees at the hospital, but they were all old men and women who had lost their limbs from diabetes or some other illness tied to aging. I hoped to meet someone who had youth and vigor to fight. Finally, I built up the courage to call Bill Johnston, the Marine who had also been in a motorcycle accident, lost his leg and returned to active duty. I dialed the number given and got him on the phone after just a few rings. Bill was curt on the phone but gave me directions and a time that he would be free in his office at CINCPAC.

The drive was only a few miles away but CINCPAC had a completely different atmosphere than the Pearl Harbor Navy base. There was much more security and I felt a sense of great formality as I made the drive past the tall standing buildings. I approached the one that Bill had described as having a series of tall flagpoles in front and found visitor parking. Hobbling on my crutches, I made my way to room 211, where I found a sign that read "Master Sergeant Bill Johnston" in gold letters on a black metal plaque.

Bill was a stout, balding man dressed in standard Marine green and black fatigues. He offered me a chair in front of his desk and we spent a few minutes talking. Bill told me about his military career and was very matter-of-fact about his accident, in which he had been sideswiped by a car while he was crossing an intersection on his motorcycle. "The bastard drove off and I had to wait for an ambulance," he said with disgust. We talked a little more but time was short and he was on duty. He offered me his home number and invited me over for dinner on Friday night. "My wife is a great cook," he said. "And she'd love to meet you." I accepted his kind offer and welcomed this new friend into my life.

Bill had an outgoing and sometimes over-the-top personality. His charm was infectious. Bill's wife, Kate, was very kind and instantly put me at ease while I was at their house. He talked about his accident and described the various "complications," as he put it. Bill had lost a vein in the "good" leg that was not amputated, as well as one of his testicles, as a result of his accident. He never questioned his desire to stay in the military and loved being a Marine. Bill talked about good and bad days, about how the smallest thing can affect how you can move around each day. "With so many moving parts and metal, it's bound to be complicated," he said. "Sometimes I even have good and bad years. Everything varies but you just keep plugging, taking one day at a time."

He went on, telling various stories about his leg. He tried to keep things light and told me that he used his leg as a prop so people would know when he was having a good or bad day at the office. "If things are really bad, I take it off and prop it on my desk near the door. When people see the leg, they know to stay away unless it's urgent." He told his stories in a playful manner but I knew there was a serious tone to it. He walked very well and said that he ran five miles a day with the prosthetic leg. "I don't let up on PT or use my leg as an excuse. I'm out there with every one of my men doing PT every morning." I was incredibly impressed and wanted to tap into Bill's energy. He gave me a new sense of drive.

CHAPTER 14
- FIJI MISSION TRIP -

Having faith is easier said than done. The first year after my wreck was by far the hardest. I was struggling physically and the battle for my independence was taking its toll on me. At times, I started to question everything. I was going through a tough phase of my life and was lucky to have a strong spiritual group at Makakilo Baptist Church to support me.

During that time, Pastor Ray Viliamu was planning a mission trip to Fiji. He was forming a small group of people from our church who could take two weeks off and fly down to Fiji to help build a parsonage in a small village.

Steve Phillips, who had become one of my best friends in Hawaii and who was one of the twelve people heading to Fiji, encouraged me to go. I had not traveled since the accident, though, and this would require a twelve-hour flight as well as two weeks in a village with limited resources. Having to be on my feet much of the time and helping to construct the parsonage presented an additional physical challenge. The idea was a bit of a stretch but I figured if things fell into place, then they were meant to be.

I first approached my doctor about going. The idea of getting me out of my routine to push the limits of what I could do intrigued him. He felt that since there were still pending surgeries, he could fix whatever I broke and he was the first to give me clearance as long as I monitored my progress and was careful not to push myself too hard. My prosthetist then provided me with the necessary supplies of socks and equipment to manage my artificial leg. His approval was an easy one.

The next step was getting clearance from the Squadron office where I was working. The *Birmingham* was at sea for its western Pacific cruise and was not scheduled to return for almost six months. Although I was contributing at the Squadron on a regular basis, my work was not critical to operations. In addition, Captain Bruce Engelhardt, who was head of the Squadron and commonly referred to as "Commodore," was an encouraging and supportive fellow Christian. He provided tremendous help and granted me the permission to go. The Commodore was a wing of support to me in place of my Commanding Officer, Mark Kenny, while the *Birmingham* was away. As luck would have it, Chief Petty Officer Gary Hockett, a member of my church in Makakilo and part of the Fiji mission crew, was also on staff at the Squadron. It helped that everyone at work knew him well and was familiar with the upcoming mission trip.

Finally, I needed to get clearance from the church. Because they were financing a significant part of this mission, each member had to be approved by the pastor and the congregation. I spent a great deal of time helping the mission team plan and organize the trip, and the other members became comfortable with me going with them. In the event of any issues, Steve and Gary said they would be happy to volunteer their assistance. Although I was nervous about getting approval, in the end it was simply a matter of the pastor nominating all the members of the group during a Sunday service and the congregation saying "aye" to show their approval. It was unanimous.

As the days approached, I became more and more excited about the trip. Since it was my first flight traveling with the prosthetic, I made sure to pack every supply I could imagine. I also decided to travel with my crutches so walking would be easier. The flight was a twelve-hour journey with a short layover in Western Samoa, just south of the equator. In addition to being in the southern hemisphere, Fiji is also across the International Date Line, so we would actually lose a day traveling over there. The flight was a redeye leaving Honolulu Airport at 11 p.m. on Sunday night. I had butterflies in my stomach starting late in the afternoon.

We all boarded the vans in front of Makakilo Baptist Church on Sunday evening around 8 p.m. A group of church members came to assist us in loading the vans and to see us off. We loaded all our gear and headed to the airport. Our group arrived at the airport, checked in with Air Pacific, and proceeded to the gate. We boarded the plane as scheduled. The airplane was well furnished with a friendly staff of attendants. After serving us dinner and complementary wine, they turned on the movie and turned out the lights so everyone could sleep. I was far too excited to close my eyes, so I passed the time reading the onboard magazine and daydreaming.

As we approached our destination, we could see the cluster of 333 islands that make up Fiji. We landed on Viti Levu, or "the big island," which houses the two largest cities in Fiji. It is also where a majority of the population resides, as many of the other islands are small, uninhabited land masses. After our plane landed, we were greeted by two local officials, one of whom Pastor Ray embraced enthusiastically, telling us that he was an old friend.

As we walked off the plane, the airport had a feeling of serene seclusion. Certain qualities of the airport, like the open-air windows and green, tropical surroundings, reminded me of Hawaii, but this airport had even fewer amenities. It was small and our plane was the only one landing that morning. We followed the crowd through customs, where we had to declare anything we were bringing into the country. I was overcome by a sense of peace in this quiet new place.

As we exited the airport, our local guides led us to vans they had prepared for our arrival. Pastor Ray informed us that his friend, the local official, was actually the Minister of Recreation and Sporting for the Fijian government. He was a longtime friend of Ray and had

99

helped to facilitate our church mission. I had never been around such a prominent figure before, and I was amazed at how down-to-earth and friendly he was. It took a while to load everything into the vans - in addition to things packed for our two-week stay, many of the other men had brought tools for the construction process that might not be easily accessible on this small island. During our ride to the village, we were handed small guidebooks about Fiji. The guidebooks had some touristry information about Viti Levu as well as some common Fijian phrases that might come in handy. Bula'ia, or Bula for short, was the Fijian greeting similar to *Aloha* in Hawaii. The literal translation means "peace" but it was commonly used in all local greetings.

The trek to the village was a one-hour journey in a European minivan that took us across open plains and roads that wound around the island, parallel to the shoreline. The narrow two-lane path that circled the entire island along the coast was surrounded by thick bush and large trees covered with greenery. Beyond the densely populated areas, Fiji was not very developed. The road that we followed was akin to something you would find in a small country town in the United States, but it was the island's major road and the only one maintained by the government. Traffic was sparse and the most common vehicle we saw was the same European minivan we were riding, one that could seat eight to ten people with room for luggage in the rear and in a compartment on top.

We would frequently pass locals walking along the street, trying to get a lift to the next town. The Fijian people had dark brown skin and had features similar to the Hawaiians and Samoans back in Honolulu. Many of them were fairly stout and were physically strong from the manual labor that was required to maintain their village. Along one turn, our driver decided to pick up a lone man looking for a lift to Suva, the next major town we were passing through. "Bula!" he said as he climbed into our van. He was quiet but courteous during the ride and thanked us with a "Vinaka!" when we dropped him off. The guy driving us explained that owning a vehicle in Fiji was not a common thing and many of the locals did not need one since most of their time was spent around their own village. Giving the local guy a ride made me feel good, like we were helping somehow. It also started building a new perspective for me, one that made me think of all the things I had instead of the things I didn't.

After our trek, which seemed to circle the entire island, we took a turn onto a road that led to the village that would be our home for the next two weeks. The small dirt road led to a gravel parking lot about 100 yards from the ocean. Across the water we could see a small island with only a handful of palm trees. Steve and I hopped out of the van and walked along the short grass field scattered with coconut trees, going right up to the ocean. I was stiff from sitting for so long, but the warm, humid air helped me loosen up quickly. The waterline approached the edge of the field and we could see the clear bottom of the ocean, covered with white sand and coral reefs as far as we could see. The sight was awe-inspiring and we were instantly filled with a new dose of exhilaration and excitement.

To the right of the parking lot sat the small group of bungalows where we would be staying. We unloaded the vans and carried our bags to the bungalows we had been assigned to. Each of the small houses was equipped with two rooms for living space, a small kitchen and a bathroom that predated anything I had ever seen before. The toilet had an archaic porcelain water tank attached high on the wall with a chain pull cord used to flush. We slept four to five per bungalow, or two or so people per room of living space. Steve and I shared a room, and we each had a small single bed against the wall on opposite sides of the room. The accommodations were modest but I would soon find out that they were luxurious compared to the tents where the village people lived.

That night, several village people welcomed our arrival and announced that we would be treated with a feast, courtesy of the local women. I was excited about our upcoming meal and hungry from the long journey, which had lasted over thirty-six hours since leaving Hawaii. We helped prepare large wooden tables in a community hall by spreading tablecloths over them and putting napkins at each setting.

When the local women arrived, they carried in large steel pots of food and placed them on a long table at the side of the room. Ray announced to our team that we would be eating a local meal of "taco." Intrigued, I wanted to ask if it was similar to the familiar Mexican dish I knew but I decided to wait and see. We stood in line, each of us armed with plates but no utensils (as was Fijian custom), and I gradually approached the large pot of food. Finally it was my turn. Inside I saw several small octopuses in a white milky sauce made from coconut milk. Unlike seafood I was familiar with, the entire octopus was still in one piece, with its head and legs attached. I asked Ray how we were supposed to eat it and with a broad smile he said, "Just tear off a leg and eat with your fingers." I tried grabbing hold of a tentacle but the octopus kept slipping through my fingers and splashing back into the pot. I grew frustrated, and my appetite started to fade. I didn't take any from this pot and walked on down the line only to learn that the other pots were filled with a similar style of cooking that didn't appeal to me. I passed on my first meal.

With no electricity in the village, there was no lighting to guide our way during the night, so we struggled along the path back to our bungalows. Tired from our long trip and lack of sleep, we all crashed soon after sunset.

The next morning, the vans came to pick us up from the bungalows. We departed for the village where we would be working, which was a few miles down the road and in an even more desolate area than where we stayed. It turned out to be a small community of three families, around eighty people total. They had a chief, who was the eldest in the village and the people's leader. The village was a field peppered with palm and coconut trees next to the ocean, not too different from where we had spent the night, although instead of bungalows, these people stayed in tents made of wooden frames and cloth exteriors. Since the temperature was warm year-round, there was not much need for shelter. The ocean provided all the seafood the village required and the farms located across the road provided them with their fruits and vegetables. Fires were prepared to cook food as necessary and almost everything was prepared in some form of coconut milk. This world was far from anything I was familiar with and I tried to soak it all in.

We began our work, building this small village a church, around 9:00 in the morning local time. The church would be located near the road at the front of the village. During an earlier mission trip that I was not part of, the same crew of people had constructed a foundation and had started building four walls made from concrete cinder blocks, and our job on this trip was to complete the walls and construct the roof. With tools in hand, each of us went to work as directed by Ray and the village chief. Many of the local young men joined our efforts and progress was made quickly.

After a couple of hours, we heard the chief's wife approaching our group, saying it was "tea time." One of the guides within our group told me that Fiji used to be a British colony. A few of the English customs, one being tea time, still remained. The British influence was also evident in the language, as many of the people of Fiji spoke English as well as Fijian. The tea time was an odd departure for me at first. I couldn't get over this bare village of tents and farmland having a break for tea each morning.

One of the young men from the village and I developed a unique friendship. He was curious about the prosthetic leg I had and I could tell he wanted to ask questions, but he didn't speak English very well. We hammered away together at the 2 x 4 wooden beams, contributing our part to the construction of the church roof. Since we spent most of the time working, the days went by quickly.

As the weekend rolled around, we were able to take Sunday off from our work in the village. Ray and one of the island guides gave us a tour of a luau pit, where they were roasting a side of pork for our dinner. The pit was a small hole dug out of the ground and the meat was wrapped in a moist burlap sack, then buried in the pit with hot stones and covered with dirt. The meat was slow-roasted all afternoon while we prepared other items for our meal.

103

Nader Elguindi

Several of the men took ropes made in the village and looped them around one of the coconut trees. After positioning the rope near the top branches, they pulled the tree down within reach so we could hand-pick several fresh coconuts from the tree. We were then taught the appropriate way to chop coconuts. Using a flat iron stuck into the ground, we shaved the husk of the coconut by stabbing the coconut into the flat end. We then tapped the soft spot on the end of the coconut so we could get to the milk inside. The "meat" inside the fresh coconut was soft and juicy, unlike the rock-hard stuff my mom had given me to try as a kid. I loved opening the fresh coconuts - this felt like real island living.

The locals shared with us how they used the coconut and its tree in many ways for living on the island. The milk was used both as a drink and for cooking, and the meat was eaten as a snack. The husky exterior of the coconut served its purpose as kindling for fires, while the leaves from the tree provided roofing shelter for tents. Even the coconut shell was used for various purposes, such as bowls or for tools around the village. I was amazed at the resourcefulness of these island people and how nothing was wasted.

Each day we observed the progress we were making on the church. Ray would take photos to document the development of the church. Toward the end of the week, the roof was almost finished. Our final task was to hoist the A-frame onto the four walls we had helped build, then secure it in place. With everyone's help, the roof was positioned and the remaining elements were completed. A sigh of relief went through our group as two weeks of exhausting work finally came to an end.

On our last day in the village, we all gathered in the building we had just finished putting together. As we took our seats in the front of the church, all the village women and men began filing in, standing in rows from front to back. There were a few chairs in the front for our group and in the back for the elderly but almost everyone else was standing. All of a sudden, as if on a silent cue, the women began singing. Their voices filled this small area, their new church. Their

104

harmonies began resonating as if they were coming from beyond the walls. Their sound so filled the room that I was given a sense of awe. These people who lived off so little, who were just happy to have roofs over their heads, and who had no formal singing lessons, had a harmony that rivaled anything I heard before.

Later that night we packed our bags and headed back to the airport for our return to Hawaii. I was leaving one paradise island behind and returning to another. I developed a new sense of appreciation for what mankind is capable of accomplishing. I learned exactly how much can be done with just the resolve of the human spirit. It fueled my fire to continue my journey and work even harder than I had before.

Chapter 15
- Back to Work -

Back at Squadron, I was required to check in with the staff doctor, Dr. Greg Moes. He was a young and upcoming physician in the Navy. He was from Vermont and had moved to Hawaii around the same time I did. Dr. Moes mentioned having heard about my story and was supportive in helping me navigate the bureaucracy of medical waivers. Because his office was in the same building where I worked on a daily basis, he was accessible when I needed him. I reported to him on occasion for updates and to give progress of my latest activities. He kept the Squadron Commodore, Captain Bruce Engelhardt who was also a strong support of my return to the boat, updated on my activities.

As time progressed, Dr. Moes informed me that I would have to start checking in with the chief medical doctor for the base, Captain Robert Murray, an older Navy medical officer located at the base hospital. Dr. Murray's office was located on the other side of the base, a short drive from the Squadron office. My first encounter with him was cordial but brief.

"I've spoken with Dr. Moes," he said. "He tells me that you want to continue working with the Navy."

"Yes, sir. I've been doing administrative work at the Squadron but would like to get back on my boat soon."

"Well, son, you'll have three chances to achieve fitness for duty." Dr. Murray explained the process of the Physical Evaluation Board

(PEB), where anyone with a medical condition who wants to stay in the military must get approval. The PEB is a board of medical officers and doctors located in Washington, D.C., who evaluate and decide whether military personnel are allowed to stay on active duty despite their medical conditions. Dr. Murray informed me that the process can be drawn out, playing to my advantage for a recovery. He looked me over. "The first filing will have to be made within one year of your accident, so I will put in for a request for extension until that time. That way I will have the rest of the year to monitor your progress."

Dr. Murray also informed me that I was only allowed three chances and if my first two evaluations failed, I would be forced to accept the result of the third finding without an option to appeal. The process appeared complicated to me but Dr. Murray said it was quite common that I would not have to appear in person to the board; rather, he would conduct evaluations on me and put his findings in writing, which would be submitted to Washington. I was eager to get on but it was slow going and responses would take up to six months. Dr. Murray encouraged me to have as much of my normal activities while onboard the boat documented so he could place that in the report. He believed that would help my case.

Back at Squadron, I learned that my boat, USS *Birmingham*, was heading home after successfully completing its Westpac cruise and special operation known as "specop." The Westpac, short for Western Pacific Cruise, entailed a six-month journey with various port stops around the world. The port stops served both as a break for the crew and boat as well as a demonstration of "power projection" of U.S. military might. Our presence in foreign countries helped establish a sense of law and world order, similar to police monitoring the city streets. During most Westpac cruises, a submarine conducts a two-month specop during the end of cruise. These highly classified operations were the golden nugget of a seagoing operation and helped maintain the U.S. Navy as the superior submarine service in the world.

When my boat arrived back in Pearl Harbor, I was standing alongside the pier, as I had the previous year when I first reported to the boat. This arrival was significantly different, since the crew had been away from port for six months. Westpac cruises generally occurred once every two years, and were considered the most significant cruise a submarine conducts during its tour. All the wives and family were standing portside along with senior staff from the Squadron, ready to greet the return of Pearl Harbor's pride from its long journey. As the boat docked, many of the men rushed off the boat, embracing their loved ones. Crew members were covered with fresh leis and flowers, just like tourists arriving at the Honolulu airport.

It was good to see my captain and friends as they disembarked the boat. The last time I saw many of them, I was still horizontal in my hospital bed. They applauded my progress and welcomed me as I welcomed their arrival. Lieutenant Commander Hankins, our chief engineer, asked in a sincere and encouraging way when I would be getting back on the boat. "We missed you at sea," he said.

I was hungry to rejoin my crew and Navy family.

My mobility had improved dramatically and I was using a cane to walk around on good days. I carried the crutches around in my Jeep for ready access, but I tried to walk as much as possible. The process to get back on my boat, though, required much more than improved walking. I had to get medical clearance to operate on the submarine, and Dr. Moes worked with me on various training exercises and tests to ensure that I could scale ladders and maneuver through narrow passageways. Submarine quarters were tight and I would not have the amenities that I enjoyed on land.

To aid that process, I would visit the boat on a regular basis. After work days at the Squadron, I would join the officers for dinner on the boat. I started finding that navigating the submarine provided some natural benefits. The narrow passages and guiding handrails provided good support, which replaced the need for a cane on the boat. Stairs and ladders were trickier, but I continued to practice as much as I could.

After a few months, Dr. Moes agreed that I needed a short test cruise so my captain and the onboard medic could evaluate my ability to get around at sea. During the summer, the *Birmingham* would be conducting a short sea cruise that would only last a few days. It presented the best opportunity for me to try things out. Commander Kenny was supportive and provided me the approval to seek a waiver. Dr. Moes signed off on its approval after going with me to the boat one day and watching me demonstrate how I got around, and, in turn, he briefed the Squadron commodore, Commodore Engelhardt. Sufficiently satisfying all requirements, I was given a temporary waiver and allowed back to sea for the first time since my accident.

Adrenaline was running through my body. "Cast off all lines," I heard through the portholes. "The ship is under way," went over the 1MC system that could be heard throughout the boat. Soon we would be at our dive point and back at sea, silently cutting holes in the big ocean. Once under way, everything went well without any incidents. Although not graceful, I was able to successfully maneuver around the boat. I found relief from standing for long periods by resting on a stool or nearby bench. Getting in and out of my bunk proved to be easy enough since I was positioned on the bottom of the three beds. The hardest thing for me to do during that short cruise was take a shower. My left leg still required the support of a small brace and I was not able to stand on it with a bare foot. The prosthetic was not waterproof, so it could not go into the shower. I accommodated my inability to shower by relying on the dry showers I learned about while bedridden at Tripler: I would sponge bathe myself at sea and cover myself with enough deodorant so I could get by for the few days away.

We arrived back in Pearl Harbor as scheduled. I was thrilled by my successful arrival back to port and departed the base that evening with a new lease on life. I knew I was on my way; now I just had to convince the world of the same.

And that world was the PEB. My one-year anniversary was coming up and the deadline for supplying my first evaluation and request for fitness was due. I reported to Dr. Murray's office and discussed my progress and recent successes. He conducted various physical tests of both my endurance and stamina. We practiced standing for lengths of time and he completed his evaluation with the support of his previous notes. Although not the glowing testimony of being able to leap tall buildings in a single bound that I had hoped for, Dr. Murray completed what I considered a generous request and one that would hopefully be approved.

Now I only had to wait.

CHAPTER 16
- SUBMARINE QUALIFICATIONS -

After returning from the short cruise, I went back to work at the Squadron. I was not yet cleared for active duty on the boat and had to stay in an administrative role until my clearance came through. The Commodore encouraged my active involvement at Squadron, and when an opening came up in the operations group, I requested reassignment to that group. My duties within the administrative department were limited, but working in the operations department would give me a good chance to improve my operational proficiency.

The ops department was run by Lieutenant Commander Guy, a twenty-year veteran of the Navy who originally started as an enlisted man before completing his degree and earning his commission. He was responsible for the planning of all missions and scheduling of the submarines attached to the Squadron. We managed the submarine scheduling based on maintenance, operations and tactical exercise. I became actively involved with the boat operations and stayed in regular communication with the seagoing teams. I learned in-depth detail about drafting submarine orders and missions as well as the navigational charting that would become an invaluable asset when I returned to the boat.

My operational experience also helped me advance my submarine qualifications. I continued to knock out the academic portions and occasionally visited the boat to conduct at-port operations or simulations for some of the onboard check-offs. As time went on, I became limited in what I was able to complete without going back to sea, but *Birmingham* was planning a ten-week cruise to San Diego and Vancouver in early January. I marked the dates on my calendar and mentioned my desire to go back for that cruise so I could complete all my quals.

Back at Tripler, I saw Dr. Ono so I could share my progress and desire to complete a two-month mission at sea. My left leg was doing well but it became apparent during the meeting that it would need one more surgery. I still required the brace and my ankle joint had started to force the foot into a permanent downward angle, causing me pain and challenging my attempts at mobility. It had to be straightened out and the angle further solidified so I could walk flat-footed and without a brace. Dr. Ono decided to schedule the surgery for a time following my return from the cruise in the spring. That gave me the needed time to complete the two-month cruise and hopefully finish my submarine qualifications.

At the Squadron, everyone was helping me get back to sea. The Commodore, impressed with my passion to continue as a submarine office and Commander Kenny's continued support, made all the right calls to get my waivers pushed through. Commodore Bruce Engelhardt was a decorated Navy officer, wearing medals that were far above what his rank usually recognized. His influence as a distinguished naval officer helped expedite the support I needed.

Back at the medical office, Dr. Moes signed off on what he needed to as well. Everything had come through and I was gearing up to go back to sea. On the boat, I was outfitted with a bed in one of the three staterooms for officers. This was a significant promotion since only the nine most senior officers (other than the Captain and Executive Officer) were given these rooms. Submarine staterooms were laid out so that three officers could sleep in one room with the bunks stacked on top of each other. Other bunks on the middle level, where the wardroom and staterooms were located, included two thirty-nine-man bunk areas for enlisted and one nine-man room that was shared by senior enlisted and the most junior officers.

Soon after the New Year, *Birmingham* went to sea. It was my first major journey on the boat since the first long sea mission, RIMPAC 94, that I was on the summer after I first reported to the boat. I was filled with excitement and anticipation, so wasted no time working my way through qualifications. Within a short period, I requalified for the Engineering Watch, as EOOW , so I could join the officers in watch rotation in the engineering spaces. The addition of a watch officer help eased the rotation for all the junior officers on the boat to one-in-four for both the EOOW and the OOD. With four watches each lasting six hours, it was a lot easier to plan and manage the schedule when there were four individuals working each rotation. Prior to my qualification, there were three guys who rotated every eighteen hours. Aside from working more, they were not able to develop a routine since the time slots they worked varied each day with a short-handed staff. The relaxed watch schedule was a welcomed relief for the junior officers and I was glad to be helping in a small way.

Since my sole purpose for the cruise was to complete my qualifications, I was not assigned a full division but was given the position of assistant navigation and operations officer, referred to as the A-Nav. My operations duty back at Squadron had improved my skills with navigational planning and the navigation officer on the boat, Lieutenant Craig Doxey, welcomed my assistance. A-Nav duty was not as time-consuming as other Division jobs, so I focused myself on completing my Officer of the Deck qualifications. Our normal "daytime" hours from 7:30 a.m. to 5 p.m. were filled with many drills, working on our at-sea proficiency as a team, but I still found time to spend on the "Conn," which is the main control room where all the driving decisions of the submarine are made. The navigation, diving controls, periscopes, sonar and weapons system were all located within close proximity of Conn, so it provided the perfect position from where the Officer of the Desk can navigate the submarine. With the various line-ups and operations conducted during drills, I was making a lot of progress with my qualifications.

Our first port stop during the cruise was San Diego, California. After more than two weeks at sea, many of the crew welcomed the break. San Diego was a favored port stop, since the nice weather and great nightlife created a perfect atmosphere for the young and single men on the boat. *Birmingham* docked at the sub base just north of Coronado Island. The weather called for sunny days in the mid-70s for the entire three days we were planning to be there. My first night in San Diego, I opted to stay on the boat. Several of my qualifications included shutdown and shore power operational jobs, which only occurred when you first pull into port. In addition, I was fatigued from being on my feet during the cruise and wanted to get some rest the first night.

On day two in San Diego, I decided to venture out. Several of my friends were going to the San Diego Zoo, which was supposed to be one of the largest in the country. I put on my shorts, grabbed my cane to assist me walking when I needed it and we headed out. We spent the day strolling around the zoo and I even caught a glimpse of the famous Panda Park, which the zoo was known for. As we were departing the zoo for the day, several of the guys wanted to pick up some items from the gift shop. I was exhausted from all the walking, so I parked myself on a nearby bench while the others shopped.

My head was down from exhaustion and I started wondering how long it would take for me to develop enough stamina for walking like a normal person. Then I heard a man's voice. "Look Joe, he's got a leg just like you." I looked up and saw a man holding a small boy's arm and pointing to me. The boy, who couldn't have been older than five, had a prosthetic foot on his right leg. It was flesh-colored and inconspicuous, and he walked well with it, but there was the hint of a slight limp. I felt an instant bond with the small boy and waved to him. He was obviously shy and looked at me with a blank stare, but eventually he smiled and waved back.

It dawned on me that this is who I would be for the rest of my life. Forever an amputee and part of another community of people in the world. Knowing that others like myself were out there was comforting. I became inspired by the young boy who was probably born without a leg. We had connected instantly through our loss.

Back at the sub, we made preparations to go back to sea. Our mission indicated that we had some training operations to conduct with ASW (Anti-Submarine Warfare) before we headed north to Canada. Similar to how we headed to sea from Pearl Harbor, we stationed the maneuvering watch in preparation for casting off from the pier. This time, I was assigned to one of my practice OOD with one of the other senior officers. My first maneuvering watch as Officer of the Deck!

When a submarine makes preparations to go to sea, the OOD, assisted by a lookout, occupies a small space in the top of the sail. Crewmen are then stationed topside to cast off lines and secure the deck prior to exiting the harbor. With the EOOW stationed in the engine room, I received the call, "The reactor is critical," which meant that we would be ready soon for steaming operations.

This January afternoon in Southern California had clear blue skies for as far as we could see and calm seas - it all made for perfect departure conditions. As the report came from the engineering spaces that everything was ready, I gave the order, "Cast off lines!" And the *Birmingham* was under way.

With the assistance of a tug, we were guided out of the tight spaces of the sub base and into the channel, which we would follow to sea. "Make turns for five knots," I called out to the helmsman, who then rang the Engine Order Telegraph (EOT) as appropriate. Since the EOOW and men in the engine room actually controlled the steam level and speed of the boat, we used an Engine Order Telegraph from the Conn to dial in what speed we wanted. The EOT was just a dial with the various standard speeds for our boat. When we turned the dial from Conn, a bell rang up with the same dial in the engine room letting the guys know what speed we wanted. Keeping a slow and steady pace, I guided the submarine down the channel and out of San Diego

Harbor. As we passed the lighthouse north of the sub base, which marked the westernmost point of the harbor, the seas started to get stronger and we could feel the rocking motion of the boat from the waves of the ocean.

Since it was such a clear afternoon, many other boats were on the water. Sailing and fishing vessels were scattered across the ocean and made navigating a nuclear submarine quite a challenge. Since we were one of the larger boats on the water and a military vessel, we had to operate at as safe a distance as possible. The smaller boats, such as the fishing vessels, made our route especially difficult. About one mile outside the harbor, I noticed a small group of fishing boats clustered together on the starboard (right) side of the channel. My lane was limited and I could not go around. I chose instead to reduce my speed to 3 knots, a mere crawl.

As the boat crept down the channel and the fishing vessels were directly off our starboard beam, I could see that they were all clustered together and pointing toward something at the center of the group. Most of their crews were topside, standing on the bow, and some people had cameras. With the use of my lookout's binoculars, I could see that there was a pod of humpback whales traveling alongside the boats. A couple of the boats were actually yachts, not fishing boats as I had suspected from afar. The people were actually just tourists enthralled with watching the whales swim by.

It was a beautiful sight to see these whales swimming in the open ocean and I started to take it all in when a giant spout blew one hundred yards in front of the submarine. The lookout and I were so distracted with the whales to the right of us that we were not paying enough attention to the channel ahead. In a panic and worried that I might collide with the whale, perhaps killing it or damaging the boat, I rang up "All back emergency" on the Engine Order Telegraph. The call was for the engine room to switch directions of the propeller called a "screw" to go backwards as fast as it could. All Back Emergency is typically used for just that, an emergency, and to stop the boat quickly.

The 7,000-ton boat began to shake violently. Much like jamming your car into reverse while driving down the street, everything started to rumble and the water behind the boat was churned into large waves of whitewash. Weighing almost 7,000 tons, the submarine does not exactly stop on a dime. With momentum still pushing us forward through the ocean, my eyes were locked in front of the boat. Water was rushing over the front of the submarine and cascading down the side of the curved hull back into the Pacific Ocean. In that instant, I saw one of the most incredible sights of my life. Pacific whiteside dolphins jumped out of the water and onto our boat as the water cascaded off the sides. There was a school of them that must have been traveling with the whales. Our submarine became an instant playground for these beautiful animals.

But the boat was still shaking violently from the reverse engines. "What the hell is going on up there?" screamed the Executive Officer over the 7MC, which was used to communicate to the OOD from Conn while he was stationed in the sail. I quickly rang up "ahead one-third" so the boat would start moving forward and tried to explain what was going on topside.

The people working on the Conn burst out laughing. Everyone got a kick out of the "I almost hit a whale," comment and the Executive Officer told me to "carry on."

We continued heading out to sea.

Chapter 17
- The Final Surgery -

After leaving San Diego, we successfully completed our ASW operations and stopped in Vancouver for another three-day port stop. From there we steamed back to Hawaii and docked back at our pier in Pearl Harbor Sub Base. I was exhausted from the journey and my body was in shambles. Although I was able to successfully function at sea, my prosthetic leg had developed a mild infection. I had gone to a clinic in Vancouver where they offered me some relief, but the infection was complicating the use of my prosthetic leg and requiring me to use my left leg more than I wanted to. I hoped that my upcoming surgery would fix the problems with my left leg so I could rely on it more.

During the cruise, I had completed all my at-sea qualifications but still had two remaining check-offs to earn my Dolphins. One of the check-offs was an infrequent maintenance evolution, which only occurs every few months. I was assured that the opportunity would soon be available. The last check-off was completing a final review with my Captain, Commander Kenny.

After enjoying a weekend of rest at my home in Makakilo, I reported back to Squadron on Monday morning. My surgery was scheduled for that Thursday, so I wanted to see if I could get my last two quals completed. When I reported to duty, everyone welcomed me back from my journey. As they greeted me, each person would brush my shoulder as if to sweep salt off it. The salty shoulder was analogous to a seaman's time at sea. I had earned respect in the eyes of my peers and felt proud that I was on my way back.

When I reported to my desk, Lieutenant Commander Guy informed me that Dr. Murray wanted to see me. I strolled to the hospital after lunch to check in with him. Shortly after I arrived, Dr. Murray informed me that the review from my first PEB was back. Anxious, I asked, "Well, what did they say?" but I could tell from the grim look on his face that it wasn't going to be good news. "You were declined. The PEB recommended that you be discharged from the Navy for being 'Unfit for Active Duty.'" Dr. Murray said it was common to be declined after the first request. "It had to be filed within twelve months of the accident, so you did not have the benefit of full recovery," he continued. Dr. Murray was banking on additional time for me to get healthy in order to achieve some goals that could be well-documented for his report.

I thanked him for giving me the news and returned to my desk. I had just completed a two-month operation. I had worked so hard to get this far and now some stupid bureaucrat sitting in a soft leather chair 6,000 miles away in Washington, D.C., was determining my future.

I wasn't good enough.

Thursday came around quickly and my focus was on my final surgery. I tried to stop thinking about the PEB and focus instead on getting my body back to normal, or at least as normal as it could be. I checked into Tripler Hospital in the morning and the nurse wheeled me around to the OR where I was propped up on a gurney. Things started to look exhaustingly familiar. This was more than my twelfth time going under general anesthesia.

The technician came around and began to brief me on what he was going to do. "I've been through this a few times," I said. We joked around and I started to relax. Just as before, oxygen started flowing through the mask. I was becoming sedated and tired. Soon I would be asleep and wheeled into the OR for surgery to reconstruct my left leg. Dr. Ono had explained the plan to me during a visit earlier that week. He was planning on re-breaking the ankle in my left leg, then, using bone chips, he would form a fusion procedure called a triple arthrodesis. The fusion would join my leg bones, ankle, heel and tarsals together into one bone that would hopefully provide me enough stability to stand and walk without difficulty.

When I woke up, I found myself in the observation room where I usually stayed after surgeries. I was still groggy, just having come out of deep sedation. My left leg was wrapped in a plaster cast just as my right one had been after the major surgery when it became clear that it had to be amputated.

I panicked.

With every second that ticked by, I was waiting for the excruciating pain to kick in as it had before, but, as time passed, it didn't. I slowly began to relax. Finally, a nurse came by and said, "Everything went fine. The doctors said it was a success." I was overcome with relief.

The nurse wheeled me to a room back on the orthopedic ward, and shortly thereafter, another nurse came in to check on me. "I have your medications," she said. The doctor had prescribed Demerol, a narcotic, to help with the pain following my surgery.

I stared at the Demerol that she put on my bedside table, remembering my promise to myself. Just as she was leaving, I called after her. "Nurse! I don't need this. Could you please get me some Advil?" The nurse was surprised and asked if I was sure. "I don't need narcotics," I said. "I don't want the dependency." I remembered too clearly what it was like to be dependent on drugs. I never will be again.

I found that after the first few hours, the pain became relatively manageable. The Advil helped with the soreness and I was able to get up and around in a shorter time than expected. That night, I was joined in my room by another patient. Although a small curtain separated our bed, I could see that his head was in a metal traction. A large cage of rods sat on top of his shoulders with pins drilled into six corners of his head. One of the staff nurses informed me that he had been in a surfing accident and had broken his neck but we didn't know anything else. The man looked young, maybe about my age, but was in great shape. He looked like one of the Marines or Navy Seals I saw jogging around base. But he didn't move.

I heard his family shuffling in and out the next day and could tell everyone was glad he was alive. After a few days passed, he managed to move to an upright position. When no one was around, I struck up a conversation. He was in fact a Marine. While surfing one day with some friends he had been pummeled by a wave and his head had been shoved onto the floor of the ocean, cracking his spine. They had to fuse his neck together, and although there was no nerve damage, he was to remain in traction for several months. He said that he felt fortunate and remained positive about his recovery.

I came to realize just how close we live on the edge; you just never know what will happen. Life is too short to take for granted.

Chapter 18
- Earning My Dolphins -

Dr. Ono recommended I stay at the hospital for at least ten days following my final surgery. It would take one week before they could remove the plaster and fit me with a walking cast. With this leg out of commission, my mobility was limited to a wheelchair. The hospital environment provided the facilities for me to get around and, since the stay was short, I didn't mind.

The day before I was scheduled to meet with Dr. Ono so he could fit me with a walking cast, the Executive Officer from USS *Birmingham*, Lieutenant Commander Tim Berstch, walked into my room. "Hey, what's up?" I asked, surprised by the visit. We chatted for a little bit and Tim asked how my surgery went. After a short time of chatting, he asked, "Where is your qual book?" I kept the qual book, my career treasure, close at hand and had brought it with me in a small backpack. As I handed it to him, he said, "So I understand you have a few more steps." I agreed, letting him know the two specific check-offs I was waiting for.

"Well, the Captain and I have discussed your situation. We feel you have worked hard enough for your Dolphins. I am here to sign off on your qualifications." Tim signed the last two check-offs in my book and a smile came across my face that stretched from ear to ear. My quals were finally complete!

"Report to the *Birmingham* as soon as you're capable," he ordered. "A ceremony awarding you of your Dolphins is in order!"

125

By the next week, I was back on my feet, fitted with a new walking cast on my left leg. Since the surgery was still fresh, I required the use of crutches again, but I was too excited about my award ceremony to care. We had a scheduled time, noon, that following Tuesday to meet dockside in front of the *Birmingham*. The boat was parked on one of the submarine piers at the end of the base, not far from where I had first met the *Birmingham* when I reported two years earlier. The weather was slightly overcast but it was still warm. Joined by my shipmates from the *Birmingham* and some staff members from the Squadron, I walked to the front of the ceremony where my Commanding Officer, Commander Mark W. Kenny, and the Executive Officer were standing. The wind was blowing slightly, and, in the horizon, I could see the flag on top of the Arizona Memorial waving in the breeze. I tried to hold in my enthusiasm for accomplishing a goal that I had worked so hard for. Finally, the Executive Officer called everyone to order and we started the brief ceremony.

With the help of Commander Shinego from Squadron staff, my Captain pinned the gold colored dolphins on my shirt just above my left breast pocket. Mark then said a few words to the crew and gave me an opportunity to speak briefly: "I could not have done it without each and every one of you. First and foremost, I want to thank Captain Kenny, without whose support this chance would not be possible. To my family, crew members and friends, who supported me along the way. And finally, to God, for giving me a second chance."

I was given a plaque acknowledging this significant milestone in my career and Commander Kenny tacked a gold dolphin pin on my uniform, signifying that I was officially a qualified submarine officer. I was the first U.S. naval officer to come back after an amputation and qualify for dolphins on a nuclear submarine. And for the first time in my life, I felt completely whole.

STAGE FOUR:
THE NEXT PHASE

CHAPTER 19
- FIGHTING THE PEB -

With my newfound confidence and momentum, my mission to stay in the Navy was even stronger but the road still presented many challenges. No one before me had attempted to stay on active duty as a submarine officer with a prosthetic leg, so we were all covering new ground. In addition, I still required medical attention so had to make occasional follow-ups with my doctor. The complications did not allow me to spend as much time on the boat as I would have hoped but my goals were set on the longer-term objective.

Following my qualifications in submarines, I went again to visit the head physician for Pearl Harbor Naval Base, Dr. Murray, to work on the second appeal to the PEB. Since the first report was filed I was eager to get going on a new petition. Dr. Murray reminded me that the PEB is just a group of people who evaluate medical conditions on a case-by-case basis. "We need to build a good story about why you are fit to remain on a submarine," he said. The PEB is a composition of experienced senior military physicians as well as senior line officers. This group acts on behalf of the secretary of the Navy to make determinations of fitness for duty for active members of the Navy. Dr. Murray was my liaison to this medical board evaluating my future and our only form of communication to them was his written report. The process was convoluted to me, a young officer in the

Navy only wanting to go back to work, but I wanted to do everything I could. I wanted to provide Dr. Murray with proof and documentation that I could, in fact, fully complete all my duties as a submarine officer.

On one occasion the Squadron physician, Dr. Moes, followed me to the boat to observe my ability to shim up and down the ladders of the submarine as well as move about the tight spaces of the cabin. We tried as many combinations of exercises as possible, but came short of our last idea, which was to have me ride a dinghy to the open water, jump off then swim to safety back onto the boat. That one didn't go over too well when we presented it for approval from the Commodore. However, the achievements we did accomplish were well documented and passed along to Dr. Murray for his PEB report. That second report went to the PEB in the fall of 1996, almost two years after my accident, and I was back working on the boat until the PEB decision came in.

I received notice of my second PEB results around Christmas that same year. I recall that the findings came in earlier than expected, so I was hoping for good news as I approached Dr. Murray's office to learn the results. I walked down the familiar hallway to the staff offices located at the base medical center. It reminded me of a clinical office each time I visited, with a flurry of people in the lobby waiting their turn or perhaps for a loved one. I knocked on the door, seeing the top of Dr. Murray's gray hair as he read a document on his desk. He looked up, smiled, and said, "Lieutenant, come on in. Please, have a seat." Every time I visited, he was always friendly in spite of the fast-paced environment he had to deal with.

"The results from the PEB are in," he said, getting right to the point. Dr. Murray slid a three-page report across the desk. It was tri-folded, having just come from a recently opened envelope. I read the report, trying desperately to look for the answer to my question. Sensing my inability to decipher all the information on the report, Dr. Murray said, "Bottom of the back page. I am sorry, Lieutenant, but the PEB has denied your request once again."

I was dumbfounded.

Honestly, I had full confidence that I was going to get permission to stay on active duty. I had overcome so much and accomplished what many thought was impossible. I even surpassed what I had expected for myself, but the PEB did not see it that way. I was at risk and therefore denied the right to stay on active duty.

Dr. Murray covered my options. I could appeal again, giving it one last chance, but the third time would be the final result. I had already lost two years in recovery and was falling behind my classmates with respect to advancement. In addition, there was a limited window in which I was required to perform a minimum of two years' sea time within my first five years to qualify as a professional engineer, or PNEO. That certification was mandatory for my next advancement and for me to remain a submarine officer. I was in danger of losing more years fighting the PEB without success, and, worst of all, Dr. Murray informed me that the PEB could make a decision that would require me to work a desk job instead of being able to work on submarines, which was my true passion.

I spent the next few weeks weighing my options and talking with my close friends. My family was encouraging me in a very strong way to leave the Navy and enter civilian life. They did not share my passion for the military life, but they did want the best for me in the long run. Unfortunately, my Captain, Commander Mark Kenny, was deployed when the results came back in, so I was not able to discuss it with him. However, with Dr. Murray's strong encouragement and after a couple of weeks of considering my choices, I told the senior doctor, "I don't want to risk working a desk job, so I will take my chances in the civilian world." With that final decision, Dr. Murray accepted the findings from the PEB and mailed them back to Washington, D.C. Within six months, I was medically discharged from the Navy and, sadly, sent home.

CHAPTER 20
- STARTING CYDECOR -

The decision of where I would call home after leaving the Navy was challenging for me. My mom had moved back to Georgia and was living by herself in a small town called Douglasville. She had come to enjoy her solitude and was living in an area too rural for me to even consider. I needed a town where I could find work and needed to be close to a VA medical center where I could receive care. Since the accident, my dad had moved from Massachusetts to Arizona and he started a private practice in Yuma. It was only two hours from San Diego, which I gave serious consideration to, but it was too far away from the rest of my family on the East Coast. I had cousins and other family living in Washington, D.C., so considered moving there, but I didn't feel ready for big-city living. Everything seemed so intimidating to me then. I finally decided on Charlotte because my sister lived there and because Charlotte was a town that I was familiar with. I also had a place to stay with Nellie until I figured things out, and my best friend, Brian Wallace, was living in Charlotte with his family so there were people I cared about nearby.

I moved into my sister's apartment but kept most of my belongings in storage until I could find a job and place of my own. Nellie and I started rebuilding our relationship that had been strained from the pressures following my accident. Moving in with her for a few months gave me the opportunity to be close to her again.

Finding a job and my role in Charlotte was slow at first. I had to get acclimated with the Charlotte job market and network with new people who could help me figure out what I wanted to do. I started attending the same local church where my college roommate's father was preaching, Idlewild Presbyterian Church. There, I reconnected with a friend and mentor, Bob Johnson, who had started a business called J&H Machine Tools with his partner seventeen years earlier. I approached him one day and asked if he could meet me for lunch and provide some advice. We met up for lunch that Friday at his office. He gave me a tour of his facility and plant where they set up and sold manufacturing tools and equipment. Bob drove me from his office in his Jaguar to a small deli down the street. We had lunch and I shared with him my issues about searching for a job. I was unfamiliar with the interview process since I had joined the Navy right after college. I was also not sure how to approach my leg issue with an interviewer. It was an awkward and uncomfortable topic for me and Bob shared some of the best advice that I still carry today. He said, "Be matter-of-fact about it. It doesn't affect who you are and whoever you are speaking with does not need the emotional side of it. It just is what it is."

In addition to the advice, Bob arranged for me to meet with a vice president in his company named Cindy about a new opening in their IT shop. With all the new technology of the '90s becoming available, they wanted to hire a full-time manager of information systems to help with their networks and computers. I was fairly comfortable with technology and knew that I could learn just about anything put in front of me. The opportunity to work with Bob's company seemed exciting and I prepped hard for the interview. The process at J&H Machine Tools was unique to my experience in that they provided me a Myers-Briggs test prior to the face-to-face interview. The discussion with Cindy was relaxed and easygoing and we talked about a variety of issues. Bob poked his head in at one point to say hi and, after an hour, I was excused with a "We'll be in touch."

Waiting to hear back from J&H Machine Tools was excruciating for me. It had only been a few days, but I was anxious and impatient to start my new job. I wanted the position and had always heard that you're off to a great start when you know someone on the inside. Being friends with the owner of the company seemed an in for me and I trusted Bob and his company. I was really hoping things would work out.

Almost one week to the day, I received a call from Cindy saying, "I'm sorry, but we don't think you're right for the position." She said that there were various incompatibilities with the results of my personality exam and the position she was trying to fill. Although she wouldn't get specific, I could gather that it centered around the fact that I was a stronger personality than the position required and that she thought I would get restless for additional leadership opportunities. At first, I was surprised that Bob's pull didn't come through, but I'm sure Bob had a great deal of confidence in his people and would accept whatever decision Cindy came to without hesitation. He was an excellent businessman and strong leader, so I was sure he did what he needed to do as a manager. However, I did feel like the wind was gone from my sail and found myself lost, searching for what I should do.

I started spending more time at my friend Brian's house. He was in school part-time and his hours were flexible enough for us to spend lots of time together. His parents, Bob and Sissy, also allowed me to hang around their house a lot. I often stayed for dinner and tried to help around the house. It felt comfortable there and allowed me a good mental break so I could adjust to my new life outside the Navy.

One day, I was hanging out in Brian's room in the middle of the day, not doing much of anything. Brian was in class and due to be home soon, so I was waiting on him. Reverend Wallace came home from church early that afternoon and we started chatting. He encouraged me to search harder for a job, telling me that would give me the focus I needed. "Working hard in my job is my foundation, Nader, and I know you felt that way about your job in the Navy. You'll feel the same about whatever field you choose now - you just have to get started." His pep talk was just what I needed.

My sister was also encouraging me and one day suggested I go to a class about starting your own business that was offered by the local community college. I certainly had nothing better to do and the class, which only cost $20, was an easy decision. During my recovery time in Hawaii, I had reacquainted myself with computers and even taken some programming classes offered through the naval base. I had built a few websites and become fascinated with the Internet. Computer work also offered me the ability to use skills I had without requiring me to stand on my feet for lengthy periods of time. It seemed like a good direction for my new career or, at the least, a way to earn a side income until things worked out.

The entrepreneurial class was held at one of the Charlotte public library branches about twenty minutes from my sister's apartment. I showed up early, wanting to absorb as much as I could. The teacher was a young guy named Louis Foreman, whose credentials included growing a business out of his college dorm room. He began by selling custom, embroidered t-shirts on campus and eventually was able to sell the business.

True to my talkative nature, I asked several questions during the class and opened up some discussion about e-commerce. Louis asked me to see him after class - I thought it was his way of asking me to stop asking so many questions. After class adjourned, I went to the front to speak with him. Much to my surprise, Louis informed me that he was taking over another business called Parker Athletic and wanted to know about my experience with building websites. He gave me his business card and asked that I call him to set up a meeting. I did just that and a few days later we talked about building a new e-commerce website for his business. With limited experience but a lot of research online, I created a proposal for Parker Athletic, which would be my first major project.

My next dilemma was creating a company for my new project. The following morning, I went to the federal building downtown and registered my company under the name Cydecor. Brian and I had created the name a year earlier while brainstorming for the side projects that I was doing. The combination of "Cy" from cyberspace and "décor" for design helped create the brand for my new company. Little did I know what a ride Cydecor was going to take me on in the coming years.

With a project under my belt and cash coming in to my company, I started exploring ways to network and expand my business. I joined the chamber of commerce and other local venues where professionals connected. I spent the first few months working out of my small one-bedroom apartment. I had a fairly robust HP computer and a dial-up connection from the then hot America Online. The home PC was limiting for me, so I had to start investing in new, portable equipment. I bought a new Toshiba Laptop, some web development software and a projector from which I could conduct sales presentations. Soon, Cydecor was booming with more projects than I could handle. I started subcontracting work and finding complementary business partners willing to support me. One of those companies was a graphic design firm called Spectrum Type and Art. They were a small group of talented artists, comfortable with designing on computers but eager to learn more about web development. We set up a great teaming partnership and collaborated on many early projects. As work from my apartment became more cumbersome, I approached them about subleasing one of their offices to help my business grow. It was at that point I started believing I was really building a business but had yet to hire an employee. I was the sole worker doing the sales, project management, and administration with the help of many subcontractors.

Along the way, I met two friends, Marty and Hope, who brought the technical experience I needed to help my business meet the challenging demands of advancing e-commerce. Both Marty and Hope had daytime jobs, so my meetings with them occurred after work hours. During the day, I would spend long days at the Spectrum offices and between meetings around town. Marty and Hope would often have me over for dinner then we would head into their den to discuss the latest projects and technical challenges. Marty was a great software developer. He helped me design and build systems for many of Cydecor's clients. By the summer, only nine months after I started, the company was desperate for additional employees to help manage and eventually continue to grow our clientele. I was scared to death of the mere thought of hiring an employee. I was only twenty-seven years old, just starting my new career, and could not comprehend the idea of hiring employees or managing payroll and the other responsibilities that came with it.

I counseled with several friends and entrepreneurs along the way. Eventually Hope offered the best idea - she suggested I hire her part-time, so I could get comfortable with the idea then expand from there. Hope was already supporting Cydecor as a subcontractor, so she knew the business and tasks required. It also worked well for me since she did not have to give up her other job whiled I learned about the tasks of payroll. After a few months, I was encouraged by our progress and became comfortable with the idea of having a payroll, so I hired Cydecor's first full-time employee. It was a bit more risky for me, since it meant someone's income was dependent on Cydecor's business; however, the business climate for technology companies was fairly strong and sales for our company were coming in at a regular pace.

With two employees working full-time, one part-time and a handful of contractors, I needed to search for more office space. I felt Cydecor needed its own identity and room for growth and we also needed more money to afford outfitting another office space. We settled in a small space not far from the Spectrum office, where I had first started subleasing a small office. In addition, we were adding new personnel each month to handle the growing demands of the business. That year everyone's businesses were doing well. There was a tremendous availability of funding for all types of projects and new companies were sprouting up like freshly planted crops. It was also during this time that I learned about venture capital: an industry that provides capital in the form of cash to fledging businesses in exchange for shares of a high growth opportunity.

I was eager to be part of the wave of growth and wanted the same success for Cydecor that I was seeing all around. With help from a consultant, we developed a business plan and pitched a few of these venture capital companies. Along the way, I learned about business scalability, which is terminology used by investors to determine predictable patterns of growth for a business. For instance, two plants should produce twice as much as one; therefore, if you know the cost of each plant, then you can establish a formula for cost-to-production ratios. Unfortunately, Cydecor was more of a service organization, which is very dependent on people - not something the venture capitalist considered scalable. Undaunted, we continued our growth and aggressive new business.

To help Cydecor manage our growth, I talked to an old friend, Marco Valdez, about joining our team full-time. Marco was a shipmate from my Navy days on the *Birmingham* and a resident of Reston, Virginia. He made the move to Charlotte and soon helped us take on larger projects. It was hard keeping pace with all of the new business but we had a tight-knit group of people that worked hard and long hours. I was motivated by both the excitement of growing our young company as well as the fear of failure. As we went from two to eight full-time people, our payroll and other expenses became huge costs every month. In addition, as a service business, we billed clients after we performed the work, so there was generally a two- or three-month gap from when we paid the bills until when we collected our fees. I remember that aspect of our cash flow creating an enormous amount of financial stress.

I started to show signs of fatigue as the hours worked grew longer and working weekends became a constant. At one point, I believe I went eighteen months without taking a vacation. Unfortunately, my stress translated to the office space and I was known to crack under the pressure or occasionally be short and often sarcastic. As a joke to lighten me up, my coworkers bought me a new vitamin that was marketed as a "Stress Reliever." We all got a laugh out of it.

One of the harder things in our early years was hiring and retention during the tech boom. Developers that were both talented and qualified became more difficult to find and the big companies were using all sorts of recruiting techniques to hire folks that we could not afford. Not only could we not keep up with the salaries being doled out, but large consulting companies were recruiting from our staff. I recall one especially astounding story from a young developer, Josh, who we hired right out of college. Josh did not finish his degree but started working for Cydecor full-time after his short internship proved successful. By the end of the first year, the lure of big companies became too tempting. A firm out of Atlanta offered Josh a job that doubled his salary and gave him more than $10,000 in stock options upon signing. For a twenty-one-year-old, the offer was too valuable to pass up. As a result, Cydecor lost one of its most talented developers, and sadly started a turnover trend that lasted for several months.

Somehow, in spite of the turnover and tight labor market, we kept the business growing. By the end of 1999 our staff reached eighteen employees. We were bursting at the seams and once again needed to find a larger space. Fortunately, we were able to relocate to a space in the same office building twice the size of what had been occupying. I was hesitant to sign the three-year lease but knew Cydecor needed the space to keep up with demand. Along with the new space, we bought an additional $70,000 worth of new furniture and computer equipment. My investment in Cydecor committed us to the business plan at hand for several years to come. The large financial commitment weighed heavily on my mind. Upon reflection, I am amazed at how everything started from a project at Parker Athletic.

With a newfound identity and the confidence that a larger space offered, Cydecor hit a streak of good luck and landed two of the largest projects in its short history. One of the main issues that came up on a day-to-day basis was utilizing and managing everyone's time. As a service business, our monthly profits and success were dependent on ensuring everyone stayed busy. These larger projects added a backlog of four to six months of work, which allowed me more time to find new work.

In March of 2000, just two months after we moved into the new office space, the NASDAQ stock market crashed in what history now refers to as the bursting of the tech bubble. Many of the high-tech companies that were free-flowing with cash and resources started to struggle. Most of Cydecor's clients were not these particular high-tech companies, so at first, we did not notice a change. However, a few months after the "bubble burst," in late summer, many of our clients' investments started to falter. This translated into our clients cutting back on funding for projects and an uneasy climate, which made finding new work much more challenging. The change was not noticeable on a daily basis though; we were still meeting with prospective clients, doing presentations, and starting new projects. However, over three or four months we could tell things had started to slow down.

The hardest thing for me to recognize was how to cut back expenses. All of my office furnishings were fixed costs and I was locked into a three-year lease. The majority of Cydecor's full-time personnel were working on at least one or two projects but fewer than the three to six needed for Cydecor to keep a consistent profit. As with many young business owners, I reacted too slowly. Many of the staff had become personal friends, so there was also an emotional element to the decision. I waited as long as I could, drawing on my loan from the bank to keep payroll going. It did not seem like a bad decision at the time, since it was normal for us to make payroll then collect on the fees for billing our consultants within two or three months. The negative cash flow was part of our standard operating practice, but this time, the fees weren't coming in after payroll. We weren't billing enough fees, so when my $100,000 line of credit was maxed out, I had to start laying people off. It was one of the hardest things I have ever had to do as a business owner. In retrospect, I could have handled the whole situation much better. By the fall of 2000, I had laid off half our staff and Cydecor went from eighteen to nine employees in just two months.

Adversity continued to strike as we entered 2001. Daily news reports were filled with stories of bankruptcy that highlighted the greed and scandal of companies such as Enron and many others. Each month there appeared to be another multi-billion-dollar bankruptcy. Then, in September 2001, the unimaginable happened - the United States was hit with the worst terrorist attack in our history. Our consulting business seemed to come to an abrupt halt. Suddenly, no one was interested in talking about new projects. It took months before things even picked up slightly, so Cydecor cut its staff to the bare minimum and we did all we could to survive as a company.

That winter, we held another board meeting with four of my closest advisors. Cydecor had managed to stay in business and our revenues were still coming in, but our debt had skyrocketed to over $200,000. I was taking a minimum salary of $24,000 a year so the company could stay afloat and was working every minute that I could stay awake. I desperately wanted to determine a way for the company to survive. During the board meeting, we discussed the idea of filing for bankruptcy but I could not bring myself to seriously consider it. My determination combined with the fear of failure as well as uncertainty of what else I could do, kept me focused on finding ways to dig Cydecor out of the hole we had created.

Since new projects were not flowing in quickly enough, I decided to get creative. We had a beautiful office space with twelve offices that could fit almost twenty people. Using ideas from commercial real estate agents, I started marketing Cydecor's office space to fledging companies. We had the location, space, furnishings, phones and infrastructure many companies needed. Therefore, over the next year, I brought in two companies to share our space as sub-tenants. The income generated from the subletting helped offset many of the fixed costs I had to pay each month. In addition, working in close proximity to our new tenants allowed Cydecor to assist with their websites, software development and marketing programs. We were generating revenue from consulting with them and it was just enough to keep the doors open and our business afloat.

With a good bit of luck and a lot of hard work, Cydecor remained profitable. The threats had not all been eliminated though - the coming years presented a new challenge called IT outsourcing.

Advances in technology and the ease of connectivity to people world-wide made many businesses open their eyes to the advantages of low-cost, international high-tech labor from markets such as India and Asia. Furthermore, the tight labor market and high cost of domestic talent motivated many managers to eagerly pursue this new trend of outsourcing their software development.

Competing with outsourcing, Cydecor struggled to keep pace with its competitors and looked for a new avenue to develop business. In the middle of 2002, we decided to sell content management software products in addition to our service business. The benefit of product sales was that it provided a good way to get our foot in the door with a tangible product and also offered good margin without the high labor cost. Although product sales helped us get in the door with many new clients, the revenue that first year was not as strong as I had hoped. Business was solid but it was not quite the home run Cydecor needed.

By early 2003, I was nearing the end of my three-year lease and looked forward to the opportunity to reduce some of our fixed cost in hopes of using more of those funds to pay down the loan balances. We moved from the building we had occupied for over five years to an executive office, one mile away in the downtown district. This new location offered single office spaces that I could add or cut month to month as needed. Therefore, Cydecor reduced its overhead by thousands of dollars each month!

CHAPTER 21

- SUCCESS IS A CHOICE -

In the summer of 2003, my cousin, Arash, married his girl-friend of eight years in her home country of Malta. Arash and I were close growing up and I looked forward to the opportunity to travel to his wedding as well as enjoy a vacation away from the constant pace of Cydecor. They had a large wedding and the guests stayed at a beautiful resort overlooking the Mediterranean Sea. On the first af-ternoon, I was sitting by the pool with everyone from the group and met one of the family friends from the bride's side, Joe Beima. Joe was a retired U.S. Coast Guard officer who spent twelve years in govern-ment contracting following his retirement from military service. Joe and I hit it off immediately and shared some stories about our service. When Joe found out I ran my own company, he told me about a program offered by the Small Business Administration (SBA) that helps veteran and minority-owned small businesses develop new work in government contracting. One of the major advantages I noticed is that government services are protected from overseas labor since all of it must be performed by U.S. citizens. I became excited about the unique opportunity and made the commitment to put my efforts into pursuing the program when I returned home.

The SBA application process was long and took over nine months but Cydecor finally achieved its certification in February of 2004. I used that success to call upon some old friends located in the D.C. area and started networking my way into the government industry.

Fortunately, I had a close friend from college, Debbie Haley, whose father, Bob Osterhoudt, worked in the D.C. area. During college, Debbie talked about her father's success in the Navy and on a few occasions tried to talk me into working for him. After reconnecting with Debbie, I gave Bob a call. As it turns out, Bob worked at SAIC, which is one of the largest engineering companies in the United States and has done billions of dollars in business with the federal government. SAIC had secured numerous contracts to support the government - specifically the Navy - so I was hoping they could help me with introductions to some potential Navy clients. Bob was a retired Navy captain and as I would soon learn, a stickler for promptness. We arranged for a short meeting at his office at 3 p.m. one afternoon. I recall the specific meeting time since I had a hard time finding a parking space in the very dense office complexes of Crystal City, an area near D.C. known for its large population of government and contractor offices. I was running just over five minutes behind but was hoping Bob would understand since I was traveling from Charlotte, an eight-hour drive, to see him. I finally found the office but there was no receptionist out front. After a few more minutes, I wandered the hallway looking for Bob's office. I saw him walking out and got his attention. The first thing Bob said was, "You're late!" He invited me back anyway but said he would only give me fifteen minutes.

I shared some ideas for new technologies that could help the military and requested his help marketing them. He was intrigued enough to give me more time than he originally stated, so I took that as a good sign. We ended the meeting and I felt good about the direction we were going. Bob then offered me the opportunity to share my ideas with his coworkers at SAIC. He asked me to e-mail him something, so when I got back home to Charlotte, I created a statement of work and rough draft.

It was early 2004 and the U.S. was in the throes of war in Iraq and Afghanistan. The area of opportunity I identified was training the U.S. soldiers in these foreign countries on the cultural issues and differences that exist between America and the Middle East. I believed the training for these men and women needed to be delivered via online distance learning tools using a web portal - making it accessible to a larger number of people in those regions. I put my thoughts together in a white paper and offered it to Bob via email the following week.

Bob kept true to his promise and shared the idea with others at SAIC. We exchanged some banter but we were unable to get the project off the ground. Although that particular project did not come to fruition, Cydecor made invaluable connections with others within SAIC, so I felt it was a successful start. Undaunted by my lack of initial success, I looked for other avenues to market Cydecor's services. Joe Beima and I had remained close friends since we met at my cousin's wedding and he was kind enough to arrange a meeting for me at one of the Navy support commands. It was there that I met Cheryl Tryon, who was the Small Business Advocate for that office. She was extremely helpful and liked the ideas I shared; indicating that though her command did not work with many new small businesses, she would keep our hat in the ring. Cheryl also had a friend, Genesta Belton, who filled a similar role for another Navy command called the Office of Naval Research (ONR). ONR specializes in the research and development of new technologies for the U.S. Navy. ONR refers to itself as the "Navy after Next" meaning they have helped to develop technologies the Navy plans on using twenty years or more into the future. They employed some of the best and brightest researchers and scientists to help the Navy build fascinating new technologies.

When I spoke with Genesta, she was very nice but our conversation was short. ONR had just released a new Request for Proposals (RFP) for both large and small businesses to help them with their engineering and technologies. Because of a specific rule in government procurement, ONR employees are not allowed to have one-on-one conversations with contractors after an RFP is released. The rule was implemented to prevent bias in the competition process, meaning I was unable to meet with Genesta, but I did receive a copy of the RFP. This document was the largest RFP I had been exposed to and was easily over 100 pages. For the first few hours, I just stared at it in awe. The fleeting moment of finally having arrived into government contracting was surpassed by the daunting task of addressing the proposal. In a moment of panic, I called Bob Osterhoudt at SAIC. He said, "Send me the RFP and we'll take a look."

The next call I received from Bob summoned me to get to their office outside of D.C. as quickly as possible. The RFP was due in thirty days and we did not have time to waste. I booked my flight to D.C. and was sitting in Bob's office in a matter of days.

Bob introduced me to several other members of the SAIC team who were interested in ONR. They indicated that SAIC had been trying to get "in the door" with ONR and welcomed the idea of "teaming" with Cydecor on the opportunity. Based on the rules of contracting, ONR was required to award a certain number of contracts to small businesses, so SAIC felt that our status and experience could be a benefit. SAIC agreed to help Cydecor with the proposal in exchange for a subcontracting opportunity if we were awarded the job. The great news for Cydecor was there were six or seven employees who would help write and respond to the proposal, which was an invaluable resource Cydecor was lacking.

That afternoon, SAIC led a proposal planning session where we mapped out what was required for the proposal. We conducted many of our additional correspondence via e-mail and conference calls over the coming weeks. Everyone was given specific portions of the RFP to work on. We then collected all the individual parts to form a draft, and after a detailed review, called "Red Team," we refined our proposal. SAIC used their own finely tuned proposal center resources to do the printing and production, so the final product looked very professional.

At the end of May, we presented our mutual Cydecor and SAIC proposal to the ONR offices in Ballston, Virginia. According to their notification, ONR would inform all bidders of the awarded contract in approximately forty-five days. The experienced staff at SAIC told me that it is often longer than that, especially for larger contracts. I headed back to Charlotte for the summer since I still had a consulting business with commercial clients to manage. After a couple of weeks, the anxiety for an announcement from ONR began to fade, but by mid-July I started pondering how ONR would announce the news. Around that time, I received a call from the Defense Contracting Audit Agency (DCAA). Their local representative, Neil Braun, scheduled a visit with me to review my proposal to ONR. According to the Federal Acquisition Regulation known as the FAR, DCAA had to audit my books and processes to ensure I was legitimate and could handle a prime contract from the government.

Over the next three weeks, I provided DCAA with reports, financial statements, and access to our accounting system, QuickBooks. Ironically, it was the same accounting software I had purchased for $500 when I started the company six years earlier. We had no reason to spend a lot of money on a new system, so I used it for all our accounting. Fortunately, DCAA approved the system and allowed me to generate reports for them from QuickBooks. That summer, I learned more about government accounting that I ever cared to know. But, in the end, Neil informed me that Cydecor passed the audit with only a few discrepancies to correct.

On September 9, 2004, we received the following in a letter from ONR:

> *Congratulations! This letter is to inform you that based on your submitted proposal; your firm has received an award for CLIN(s) 0006 under the ONR Request for Proposal (RFP) Number N00014-04-R-0010, entitled "Office of Naval Research Support Services FY05 Multiple Award Task Order Contract (MATOC)." An official copy of your contract has been distributed to your organization and it should be received within 7 days from the date of this letter."*

Cydecor, just like I had been, was rejuvenated. We had overcome adversity despite a huge obstacle. Ten years after an accident that nearly took my life and certainly changed my career, I was back serving the Navy again - this time as an entrepreneur and government contractor - helping those with whom I used to serve.

Truly, Success Is a Choice!

Lessons:
- The Five Functional Balances -

Each week during my peer-visits at Walter Reed, I have the chance to witness the human spirit and its awesome power. I see the destructive forces of nature and mankind - infection taking over where a roadside bomb left off - yet somehow, against tremendous odds, a determination comes from deep inside these men and women. It helps them overcome what they probably cannot fully conceive. To see their determination unfold is truly a thing of beauty and grace that inspires me beyond words.

I try to take these examples to heart and draw from my own experience to create this level of determination in my own life. The five lessons below are an attempt to give organization to that experience. They are dedicated to all of you who face similar challenges, whether due to an accident, act of human cruelty, congenital disability, or mental barrier.

Spiritual - Believe that there is more to this world than the soil under your feet. God touches all of our lives, even if we are unaware of His presence. He is with us in our times of need as well as our times of simple pleasure. My life is a testament that He looks out for us and knows our limits better than we know ourselves. The way to find Him is not to look out at the world around us; we need only to look inside ourselves and listen intently. God will always have a path in front of us - if we choose it, it will bring us back in the right direction. We only have to open our minds to see it.

Physical - Our bodies are the tools that we use every day. Just like a car, a body needs fuel, maintenance, and occasionally new tires. No matter what your physical form is, find something that exerts your body in a positive way. Leverage your own body weight to make your muscles work. Don't just do it one time - make it a fulfilling practice. Take the long way around the office building. Walk with a friend on the weekend just to enjoy the outdoors. Minor commitments give rewards that are beyond measure.

Professional -We all want to have a purpose, a guiding light. Never is that more evident for me than at work. Each year, I set five to seven goals for myself. My goals usually include at least one thing that is very difficult to achieve and at least one thing that I am guaranteed to make. I print them on paper and tack up one copy in my bedroom and another in my office. I look at them everyday and make myself spend one hour a week working toward one of those goals. Achievement is a very important part of our lives. We don't have to look to the outside world to gain that value. We can take control of achievement in our own lives by setting our own goals - ones that we truly believe in - and providing our own rewards.

Personal - For those like me who are overly focused on the professional side of life, the personal side can be easy to overlook. If you neglect the personal side of your life, though, you are neglecting what could be a source of great joy and strength. Your personal life is not only about your family and friends - it is also about giving time to yourself and whatever it is that makes you happy. Connect with the people you love regularly, not just when they need you or you need them. Get together for family dinners. Give yourself a break to travel out of town to somewhere you've always wanted to go. Your personal life can be the key to understanding how you fit within the world.

Mental - Know and believe that you are in control of your own decisions. Believe that you are not a victim of circumstance, misfortune, or abuse. Ultimately, you have a choice in what you do and say and how you act regardless of the circumstances around you. Also be aware that every choice brings consequences. Everything you do has an impact, and sometimes the consequences of those choices can be very hard to accept. Ask yourself what you must give up if you make a certain choice and accept the challenge of what lies ahead. Nothing easy is worthwhile and everything worth fighting for has lasting meaning.

You are a gift to this world. I encourage and challenge you to choose your destiny, tap the full resources of your mind, then fulfill your true potential.

Life Is a Choice!

- Nader Elguindi

153

BIO

Nader Elguindi is an expert on leadership and motivation. As a U.S. Navy submarine officer, Nader had a horrific accident that severed both his legs and caused him to permanently lose his right foot. He overcame the accident and went on to become the first nuclear submarine officer to complete his qualifications with a prosthetic leg.

After the Navy, Nader became a tireless entrepreneur and built a consulting firm, Cydecor, from scratch, acquiring clients such as Hendrick Automotive Group, Duke Energy, and BSN medical. Following the collapse of the technology market in 2000, Nader had to reinvent himself and his company once again, building from the foundation of Cydecor and venturing into government contracting.

Today he is the president of his high-growth company and is now servicing the Department of the Navy as well as other federal clients through his business. Nader is an author, motivational speaker and a peer volunteer at Walter Reed Army Medical Center.

To request a sample of Nader's keynote presentation or to schedule him for your next event, please visit www.enader.com